A
PRACTICAL VISION
OF
CHRISTIAN UNITY

INTO OUR THIRD CENTURY SERIES

The Church in a Changing Society, William E. Ramsden
Images of the Future, Alan K. Waltz
In Praise of Learning, Donald B. Rogers
Women, Change, and the Church, Nancy J. Van Scoyoc
Shaping the Congregation, Robert L. Wilson
Ministries Through Non-Parish Institutions,
        William E. Ramsden
Sources and Shapes of Power,
        John R. Sherwood and John C. Wagner
Context for Discovery, Neal F. Fisher
Paths to Transformation,
        Kristine M. Rogers and Bruce A. Rogers
A Practical Vision of Christian Unity, Jean Caffey Lyles

A
PRACTICAL VISION
OF
CHRISTIAN UNITY

JEAN CAFFEY LYLES

Alan K. Waltz, Editor

ABINGDON   Nashville

A PRACTICAL VISION OF CHRISTIAN UNITY

Library of Congress Cataloging in Publication Data

LYLES, JEAN CAFFEY, 1942–
  A practical vision of Christian unity.
  (Into our third century)
  1. Christian union—United Methodist Church (U.S.)
  2. Ecumenical movement. I. Title. II. Series.
BX8382.2.Z5L9   262'.0011'08827   81-15032   AACR2

ISBN 0-687-33330-X (pbk.)

MANUFACTURED BY THE PARTHENON PRESS AT
NASHVILLE, TENNESSEE, UNITED STATES OF AMERICA

To

Jim Lyles

Contents

Foreword

The 200th anniversary of United Methodism will occur in 1984. The Christmas Conference of 1784 is most often regarded as the beginning of the Methodist movement in the United States. That historic meeting adopted the Articles of Religion, established a polity, elected Thomas Coke and Francis Asbury as superintendents, consecrated Asbury at the hands of Philip Otterbein and others, took organizational steps, and called for a rebirth of evangelism and scriptural holiness in the nation.

As we approach the bicentennial of The United Methodist Church, we pause to reflect upon the spread of the Wesleyan "vision of holy love and vital piety" throughout the nation. In the report of the Bicentennial Planning Committee approved at the 1980 General Conference, we see these words:

> As we approach the end of our second century, we look forward with excitement and hope to the beginning of a third century in the service of our Lord. Our concern is that, through our recognition of the past and our affirmation of the present, we will be called into the future as new beings, refreshed by our experience of Christ, revived in our commitments to bring salvation, peace and justice to all of God's children, and renewed as a people of God in our own time.

The occasion of our bicentennial is a time to anticipate the future carefully and to assess ourselves seriously. Our inheritance is one of great achievement. We have seen periods of expansion in our denomination; we are now experiencing a time of contraction and retrenchment. Yet the challenge and vision are still present—to serve in the name of Christ and to spread the call to salvation and spiritual rebirth. We need to experience anew the sense of mission and purpose which filled our forebears with the power to evangelize a nation.

Again we turn to the words of the report of the Bicentennial Planning Committee: "The future is a time for new birth, and our Bicentennial prayer will be a call to new birth of the fervent spirit of Methodism, to a new birth of personal obedience to the Christ, to a new birth of creative local congregations, to a new birth of evangelical zeal, and to a new birth of our vital commitment to peace and social justice."

All pastors and their congregations have significant roles in the celebration, the search for, and the making possible of that new birth in our denomination. It is the people in the pews and pulpits of United Methodism who must reestablish our identity and purpose; who must enfuse the church with the excitement and commitment to bring its mission to fruition. We believe that through the examination of who we are as United Methodists, what we wish to accomplish, and how we choose to pursue our goals, we will find the renewed purpose and vision to accomplish our task in the name of Christ.

Into Our Third Century, a series of books initiated by the General Council on Ministries with the encouragement of the Council of Bishops, is intended to assist your reflection on and discussion of the issues confronting The United Methodist Church. The books are based on individually commissioned studies and research projects. Over a four-year period, beginning in 1980, seventeen separate volumes are being released. This book is the tenth volume in the series. Books already published are listed opposite the title page. Others scheduled for release in coming months deal with ethnic minorities, social movements and issues, financial support, professional ministry, outreach ministries, and polity.

The General Council on Ministries is pleased to commend to you this book by Jean Caffey Lyles, which deals with the ecumenical involvements of United Methodists on local, conference, and general church levels. It explores the nature of these involvements and the commitment made to Christian unity and ecumenism. The author helps us understand not only the formal movements, but the informal ecumenical activities and the reasons for participating in these relationships.

Share your response to this book with others in your congregation. Discuss it with district, conference, and general church leaders. Explore with the author the issues raised. Your response will also be welcomed by the members and staff of the General Council on Ministries.

Norman E. Dewire
General Secretary

Alan K. Waltz
Editor

General Council on Ministries
601 West Riverview Avenue
Dayton, Ohio 45406

January, 1982

CHAPTER 1

A Practical Vision

The United Methodist Church is committed to "being ecumenical" and to manifesting the gift of "Christian unity." On that point, United Methodists are widely agreed. But when it comes to spelling out the practical implications of such a commitment for the present and future life of the church, specifying what kind of ecumenical behavior is called for on the part of United Methodists in the 1980s and beyond, strong differences of opinion emerge. These differences are not likely to be resolved in the decade of the 1980s.

That conclusion, and others I will mention shortly, are based on my impressions as a journalist who has listened to United Methodists for several months.

In an effort to learn the attitudes that now prevail in the church toward ecumenism and Christian unity, I talked with active lay people, pastors, bishops, district superintendents, clergy in specialized ministries, general agency staff people, seminary faculty, and professional ecumenists. The interviewees included men and women, persons of various ethnic groups, people from all regions of the United States. In interviews by phone and in person, in informal conversations, and in discussions at various denominational and ecumenical gatherings, dozens of United Methodists talked about the situation in their local areas. They talked about their own experiences with other denominations, about their attitudes toward different kinds of ecumenical involvements, and about their vision of Christian unity for United Methodists.

In all parts of the country, I heard reiterated the conviction that United Methodists are historically and theologically an ecumenical-minded denomination. Some recalled Jesus' prayer (John 17:20-23) "that they may all be one"; they cited key passages from Ephesians ("one Lord, one faith, one baptism"); they spoke of John Wesley's openness, his spirit of catholicity. They pointed out that United Methodists had been involved in the formative stages of the World Council of Churches, the National Council of Churches, and the Consultation on Church Union (COCU). They recalled the denomination's notable ecumenists of the past such as John R. Mott, a layman who, in his lifetime, was thought to be Methodism's greatest contribution to the ecumenical movement; and they spoke warmly of some current ecumenical leaders. They mentioned some tragic schisms in their church history that had been healed by reunion, and they discussed the 1968 merger of Methodists and Evangelical United Brethren which had created The United Methodist Church.

But along with this theoretical commitment to Christian unity, the United Methodists interviewed revealed several notable characteristics when they began to talk about existing ecumenical involvements.

1. Most immediately evident is the fact that United Methodists' primary motivation for acting ecumenically is nearly always pragmatic, rather than theological. The people of this denomination initially tend to do *whatever* they do in any ecumenical enterprise for two very practical reasons: (a) It needs to be done; and (b) "We can do it better together than separately." Then in the midst of doing it, or even afterward, they discover or invent a theological rationale for the action. That characteristic ecumenical pragmatism is essentially the theme of this book. And as we shall see, that clear-eyed practicality of United Methodists is not necessarily to be seen in a negative light.

2. The large majority of United Methodists, laity and clergy, are not very interested in organic union with other Christian

bodies. Efforts toward that end remain the special enthusiasm of a tiny committed minority.

3. Institutionalized forms of ecumenical cooperation such as the National Council of Churches and the World Council of Churches have been on the scene long enough to be accepted as givens, and there seemingly is not a large proportion of members who would want the denomination to withdraw from them. At the same time, they are regarded as being somewhat out of touch with local constituencies. Only when one of these organizations is involved in controversy that draws sensational media coverage do local church people have any awareness of their existence.

4. The ecumenical scene is most lively at the neighborhood and local community level, where church people come together in efforts to address local issues, meet community needs, or solve immediate crises.

5. The middle level of ecumenical cooperation (district, annual conference, metropolitan, or state) is most problematic, and though exceptions can be found, it is the level where funding and morale are in most serious trouble.

6. Whereas once the Christian community was thought of in terms of a twofold division—Catholic/Protestant—now United Methodists see three divisions: Catholic/mainline Protestant/evangelical. In some localities, United Methodists are finding evangelicals to be more open and cooperative than in the past, but generally, the practical meaning of this new perception has not yet been worked out.

7. The remainder of this century is seen as a difficult time for churches, an era of shr)nking resources. United Methodists have not actually decided what that will mean for ecumenism. Will there be more sharing of facilities and resources across denominational lines? Or will churches pull back on ecumenical commitments for the sake of congregational and denominational survival? Most churches are not feeling the crunch yet, but they expect it to come; they know they will have to deal with it sooner or later.

8. The possibilities for local ecumenism vary enormously from place to place. One cannot discuss United Methodist attitudes without considering the attitudes of other denominations, the local mix of religious groups, and the impact of other social forces—secularity, for example. United Methodists, perhaps more than other religious groups, tend to be "chameleons." That is, they react to the particular context in which they find themselves, either by taking on some of the characteristics of the dominant group, or by standing over against it and asserting more strongly a distinctive identity of their own.

9. Generally speaking—and this applies to other denominations as well as United Methodist—a church tends to behave more ecumenically when it is one of the smaller groups than when it is the largest one.

10. Personal factors are of great importance in all ecumenical endeavors. On the world level or in the neighborhood, nothing happens without strong, committed, persuasive leadership. The whole history of the ecumenical movement is in some sense the story of the strong personalities of its leaders.

11. Despite articulated commitments to Christian unity, ecumenism is not a top priority for The United Methodist Church. When hard choices must be made, time and money for ecumenism almost always lose out to denominational and congregational causes.

The findings of this project probably will not be startling or unexpected to close observers of The United Methodist Church. Few surprises will be found here. The learnings largely verify, rather than disprove the hunches of one who is familiar with United Methodism.

For the sake of authenticity, and to give the reader a sense of United Methodists' actual attitudes toward ecumenism, many direct quotations from tape-recorded interviews have been included. The reader should understand that some comments are more representative of a consensus of thinking within the church than are others. But even those that express an uncommon or a minority viewpoint reflect not only the speaker's personal opinion, but suggest also the thought of a particular segment of United Methodism.

It is my hope that this book may make some small contribution toward encouraging United Methodists throughout the connection to engage in serious consideration of the meaning of the mandate to Christian unity, as the Methodist movement in America enters its third century.

Acknowledgments

This book could not have been written without the help of a great many people. Thanks are due, first of all, to the General Council on Ministries of The United Methodist Church for its support of the project; to Ezra Earl Jones, who helped enormously in the initial task of defining the scope and direction of the book; and to Alan K. Waltz, a patient and understanding editor whose criticisms and suggestions were invaluable, as were his tact and good humor. My thanks go also to Mildred Griffiths and Lola Conrad of the council staff, who prepared the manuscript for submission to the publishers. Robert Huston and his staff at the General Commission on Christian Unity and Interreligious Concerns were generous and helpful in sharing their insights during the formative stage of the project. Dozens of United Methodists around the country gave of their time and freely expressed their ideas and opinions in interviews. Since they were promised anonymity in return for their candor, I cannot thank them by name here, but my gratitude is no less genuine for that. Thanks are due also to friends who opened their homes to me on my travels. And much appreciation is owed to my colleagues at *The Christian Century* for their generosity and understanding during those months when I virtually abandoned the writing of editorials to concentrate on writing this book.

Finally, thanks to my stepson, Marquis, who cheerfully

tolerated the fact that our always chaotic household was somewhat more chaotic than usual for the duration of the project. Many thanks to my husband and best friend, James, to whom this book is dedicated. He prodded, cheered, inspired; shared his perceptive insights into United Methodism; gave wise counsel, constructive criticism, unsolicited advice, and emotional support; and generally encouraged me to believe that it was possible to write this book. All this was necessary for the author's sanity, and most of it came via telephone, during a time when our respective vocations necessitated the loneliness of long-distance marriage.

CHAPTER 2

Defining the Terms

The word *ecumenism* comes from the Greek *oikoumeme*—literally, *the whole inhabited world.* In accepted usage, *ecumenical* refers to the largely twentieth-century movement directed at breaking down the barriers that separate Christian churches, and seeking Christian unity.

However, the word has come to be used rather more loosely among United Methodists to denote also any kind of common activity engaged in by Christians of different denominations, or even by persons or groups of different faiths.

As Robert Huston, chief ecumenical officer of the denomination, points out, this term has lost much of its precision and has even come into secular usage to mean "doing anything worth doing, and doing it with anyone who will do it with you." For him, the last straw in the corruption of the word's original meaning was added when the film *Network* referred to a radical guerrilla group called the Ecumenical Liberation Army. In an article in the publication *Ecumenical Trends,* Huston proposes recovering *ecumenical* in its original sense by substituting for a time the term *Christian unity* to make clear what is at stake: "If we could recycle the word 'ecumenical' so it would once again mean all action and being which we are called to perform in order to manifest the oneness of the Christian Church that has been given in Jesus Christ, the result would be quite salutary."

The denomination's General Commission on Christian Unity and Interreligious Concerns prefers the word *interreligious* when referring to relations with persons of other faiths. In the United States, this most commonly would denote

Christian/Jewish relations, though there are the beginnings of dialogues with Muslims, Buddhists, and members of other world religions. Thus *ecumenism* is reserved for relations with other *Christian* bodies.

The General Commission's guidelines for the local church defines four kinds of ecumenism:

• *Spiritual Unity:* "concerned with basic attitudes and will. . . . Do we think of ourselves primarily as United Methodists or as Christians? . . . Tacit recognition of the gift of oneness is important, but more is required."

• *Church Union:* the seeking of "visible unity" of Christ's church. Currently, that effort is focused in the work of the Consultation on Church Union, a long-term negotiation to bring United Methodists and nine other denominations into some form of structural unity. There are some scattered efforts at local church union as well.

• *Conciliar Ecumenism:* the cooperative work of councils of churches and other such organizations—at city, state, national, and world level—to carry out a variety of aspects of mission more effectively. Local ministerial associations also are included under this heading.

• *Coalitional Ecumenism:* generally ad hoc temporary cooperative efforts to respond to particular needs and issues. Sometimes coalitions that spring up to fight one battle or to deal with one emergency evolve into permanent fixtures on the ecumenical landscape, involving themselves in a wider range of problems and issues.

There are other classifications of the varieties of ecumenism. Walter Muelder, author of the 1978 World Council of Churches document "A Comparative Study of Twenty-One North American Churches on Church Unity," employs a somewhat similar division:

• *Consultation/union Model* (as in COCU)
• *Conciliar Model*

- *Coalitional Model*
- *Confessional Model* (for United Methodists, the World Methodist Council)
- *Limited Mutual Recognition.*

John Fischer, executive director of the Wisconsin Conference of Churches, describes three categories of ecumenism:

- *Ecclesiastical Ecumenism:* denominations merging or joining in some institutional fashion
- *Theological Ecumenism:* efforts at understanding one another theologically—as in Methodist/Catholic and Methodist/Lutheran dialogues
- *Functional Ecumenism:* "working together to accomplish things you couldn't accomplish by yourselves."

In talking with United Methodists, one finds *ecumenical* used frequently to mean both "open, cooperative, willing to engage in collaborative efforts across denominational lines," and "accepting other churches . . . the opposite of narrow or exclusive."

Some laity find *ecumenism* and *ecumenical* to be somewhat unfamiliar terms. Some pastors try to avoid using these words if they suspect that the laity is "turned off" by them—either because of unfamiliarity or because the terms are associated with the World and National councils of churches, or with COCU, for which some local church people have no great love. Such pastors may refer to their cooperative efforts as *interdenominational* or simply as *churches working together.*

"Oftentimes," says one pastor, "we're speaking in an unknown tongue as far as the laity are concerned. Obsession with semantics at the national level is a substitute for mission—it's easier to talk about ecumenism than to practice it."

Others are uncomfortable with attaching the word *ecumenism* to pragmatic kinds of cooperation, or to parishes and ministries united out of economic necessity. They prefer to reserve the term for efforts motivated by the commitment to

Christian unity. In speaking of churches' cooperative ministries to aid victims of famine and earthquake, a black layman says, "We support those kinds of efforts, but we don't think of them as being ecumenical as much as we think of them as being efficient. It makes sense to go where you can get it done quickly and cost-effectively." Since most United Methodists see pragmatic elements in anything that is done ecumenically, such a criterion would drastically curtail use of the term.

A conference staff member distinguishes *ecumenism* from *interchurch cooperation:* "Ecumenism is the conviction that we really are of the same cloth and that the threads need to be woven together again. That's not the operative principle at the state level, or even in the local scene." A hospital chaplain says, "What we do is *ecumenism* when there is a spirit of oneness. It's *interfaith* when we're just working together. We're stronger on *interfaith* than on *ecumenical.*"

Finally, the guidelines document referred to earlier insists that "to be ecumenical does not mean just getting together with people of other denominations for a service or activity. To be an ecumenical one, an activity *must lead to the full unity of the church*" (emphasis added).

By and large, however, United Methodists continue to attach the term *ecumenical* rather indiscriminately to all kinds of relationships with non-United Methodist Christians, whatever the motivation or ultimate goal. We will therefore use the word in that broad sense throughout this book, and we will use *interreligious* to apply to relations with non-Christians.

CHAPTER 3

An Ecumenical Self-Image

United Methodists see themselves as being open, ecumenical-minded, cooperative, and appreciative of heritages other than their own. As evidence, they cite the fact that they recognize the validity of the ministries and sacraments of other Christian traditions; they accept, without reordination, duly ordained clergy from other Christian bodies who transfer into the United Methodist system. In some areas, they have "yoked" parishes or federated churches or union churches which relate to both the United Methodist structure and some other denomination; these may be served by a minister of any one of the participating bodies.

United Methodist congregations accept the baptisms of Christians coming to them from other denominations. They practice "open" Communion, inviting to the Lord's Table "all people who intend to lead a Christian life," as the direction in the *Book of Worship* indicates. There is considerable evidence also that most United Methodists feel quite comfortable receiving Communion in a service of another denomination (though most probably would refrain in a situation where they were not sure that open Communion was the custom). The denomination's hymnbook is ecumenical in that it borrows a wealth of texts and tunes from other heritages, including Roman Catholic, Lutheran, Anglican, Presbyterian, and conservative evangelical.

In almost any town or city where cooperative church ventures are underway, United Methodists can be relied upon to be one of the groups most actively participating. Among the executives and other top leaders of local and state councils of churches, many United Methodists can be counted. On the staffs of the World and National councils of churches and the Consultation on Church Union, United Methodists are in key leadership roles.

"About anything that's going on around here ecumenically, we're in on it," boasts one pastor. And a laywoman declares, "You know, I believe we're really about the most ecumenical and open of all the churches." A southern clergyman points out that such a self-image may be indicative of the sin of pride; he says, "There is a spirit of triumphalism in our more-ecumenical-than-thou attitudes."

Others are less confident as to how truly ecumenical United Methodists are. A bishop comments, "We are as ready as any to appear on the surface ecumenical. We pay our share. We readily accept 'most any document that comes out. But we haven't developed an adequate concept of the church against which to measure this." The implication is that the church needs a well-defined identity and that United Methodists must know "who they are" before they can responsibly engage in ecumenical dialogues to explore differences and commonalities.

Another bishop suggests that for the United Methodist Council of Bishops, as well as for every other level of church life, "ecumenism always turns out to be at the bottom in terms of priorities."

United Methodists are the second largest Protestant denomination in the United States. In areas of the country where they are strong, there are some indications that they feel less need to cooperate than do smaller groups. They are big enough to "go it alone."

A clergywoman calls the attitudes that prevail where the denomination is strong, Methodist chauvinism. A campus minister suggests that "many tend to put being a United Methodist ahead of being a Christian." And a laywoman declares, "We are so big we don't need anyone—we think. Oh, it's so much more efficient, easier to go ahead and do it ourselves. We have the resources." Pausing, she adds, "But you know, we don't really."

It has been noted by more than one observer that United Methodists, as well as some other Christians, sometimes show the low priority they place on ecumenism by the representation they send to ecumenical meetings. If other denominations are represented on a council or committee by powerful leaders who know ecumenical politics and have the authority to make decisions, while United Methodists send an inexperienced person who lacks both the knowldge and political acumen for that arena, then The United Methodist Church is perceived as not taking the involvement seriously. In many ecumenical situations, a top leadership representative from another denomination would be a white, male, over-fifty bishop. The United Methodists might send instead a woman, an ethnic minority, a layperson, or a younger person, seeking to bring these folks into a more active role. Unfortunately, the denomination's good intentions may be misunderstood.

It appears that though United Methodists are ecumenical, they are not deeply and thoroughly committed. But how do others regard United Methodists? Persons of other denominations also have opinions to offer.

A United Church of Christ clergywoman who has worked closely with United Methodists in both campus and parish ministries says, "When you're really big, like the United Methodists are, the tendency is to say, 'Oh, of course, we're all for cooperation. We invite *you* to cooperate with *us*.' And I haven't seen any great change in that. If you're a Methodist, you're a Methodist first, last, and always, and it's hard to put ecumenism at a very high priority, though they give lip service to it."

A United Church of Christ clergyman who has been the executive of ecumenical agencies at metropolitan and state levels finds that United Methodists are "our biggest supporters financially" and that ideologically and theologically, they are committed. However, he adds, "Because of their size, they have a tendency to want to throw their weight around. They're big enough that if they wanted to, they could get out and go it alone."

An ecumenical officer of the southern-based Presbyterian Church in the United States, David Taylor, was invited to speak to the United Methodist General Commission on Christian Unity and Interreligious Concerns on the way United Methodists are perceived by "an ecumenical colleague in a sister church." He conferred with colleagues in a number of churches and brought a report with mixed findings. He stressed the high quality of the leadership United Methodism has given to the ecumenical movement, expressed admiration for "a marvelous blend of evangelical zeal and social passion," and remarked, "God has abundantly blessed you in numbers, in resources, and in influence."

But it was on the matter of interdenominational cooperation that he voiced the sharpest criticism, seeing a lack of "ecumenical seriousness." He offered two examples in which the denomination "really rocked the ecumenical boat." These were (a) the decision to withdraw from United Ministries in Higher Education (at the time it became United Ministries in Education) and reestablish a denominational program of campus ministries; and (b) the decision by the 1976 General Conference which required that the elected staff of all United Methodist general church agencies be members of the denomination.

Taylor believes these decisions to be related to the size of the denomination. "United Methodists are successful and success tends to self-sufficiency." He suggested that a process be devised for reviewing all the denomination's programs in terms of the church's ecumenical commitment. "It is a natural tendency in churches for programs to become more and more sectarian, if they are not regularly seen in ecumenical context." (For example, is evangelism merely the recruiting of more United Methodists?)

But if persons in other denominations have formed opinions as to the depth of the United Methodist ecumenical commitment, so United Methodists have reached judgments regarding the ecumenical openness (or lack of it) in other bodies. They are critical of churches they see as "narrow," "stand-offish," and "uncooperative." They express a certain degree of hurt and anger at the rejection they experience from some sister churches.

At the local level, United Methodists seem most frequently to work together with congregations of the United Presbyterian Church, the Presbyterian Church in the United States, the Christian Church (Disciples of Christ), the Episcopal Church, and the Lutheran Church in America. These are the denominations with which they say they feel most comfortable. Many observe that these are the churches where they would feel most at home if they were not United Methodist. Says one pastor, "I could very easily be a Presbyterian or an Episcopalian. Theologically, we're no different. The only thing about the Disciples that would be hard for me would be not being able to use anything but baptism by immersion."

Southern Baptists, Churches of Christ, Mormons, Roman Catholics, and Missouri Synod Lutherans are among those most often mentioned as being uncooperative (though there are always exceptions). A typical comment about Southern Baptists: "The Baptists are strong. They don't need anybody else. In places where they're not strong, they're more ecumenical." It is a common theme in the remarks that in areas where a denomination is dominant, it feels less need for others and tends to believe that it has the resources to do whatever needs to be done on its own; or if it does cooperate, it may seek to stipulate the terms. Says a Mississippian, "It's still basically to 'co,' while they 'operate.' "

Prominent United Methodists tell, with chagrin, stories of having been invited as special guests to Roman Catholic "ecumenical" events, but then having been ignored when Communion was served: "It was good to be together. We declared our unity, but there was nothing to indicate that we are ever going to be any more graciously received at the Table of the Lord in the Roman Church than we were before."

An ecumenist explains: "For Catholics it's a big deal to talk about Communion with other churches. The reason United Methodists see it as no problem is that they have no strong doctrine of Communion, or any sense that the liturgical, eucharistic life of the church is central. And there we have a situation that can't easily be overcome."

But if *ecumenism* means something more than cooperation among a few of the more like-minded Protestant denominations, United Methodists will need to continue to make efforts to build relationships and to break down the barriers that separate them from those Christian churches that do not practice open Communion, or that seem exclusive or narrow in other ways.

United Methodists regard their own church as having many gifts to offer ecumenically because of distinctive emphases or notable characteristics. Not all these attributes are necessarily *unique* to United Methodism; some are characteristic of other bodies as well:

• Connectionalism, the connective network of accountability. The church's structure is functional; it is organized to achieve mission.

• Commitment to education, seen in the many colleges the denomination has founded and to which it maintains a relationship.

• Recognition of women's gifts, demonstrated in the ordination and appointment of an increasing number of women to pastorates and other ministries, the increasing number of female district superintendents, and the election of the first woman bishop.

• Racial inclusiveness, shown by the many ethnic minority members whose talents are being employed in leadersip roles.

• The itineracy, the system of clergy deployment. The pastor is appointed by the bishop rather than hired or fired by the congregation, as in many denominations that use the "call" system. This has the advantage of putting the troops where they're needed. Pastor and parish give up a measure of freedom, but gain security in return. In theory, at least, every pastor has a church and every church has a pastor. Changes in pastoral leadership can be graceful transitions, accomplished without the trauma that sometimes accompanies the process in denominations where the congregation alone makes the decision.

• Freedom of belief, as contrasted with creedalism. Because the range of acceptable theological belief in the denomination is very broad, there is room for many under the United Methodist umbrella of theological pluralism.

• The "warm heart," the denomination's historic emphasis on religious experience.

• Social concern, expressed in action and service.

United Methodists also admire or appreciate the particular gifts they see in other traditions:

• The Southern Baptists' evangelical fervor and their emphasis on study of the Bible, as well as that denomination's burgeoning growth. (The admiration here is understandably tinged with envy!)

• The Disciples' passion for Christian unity and their tenacious commitment to church union efforts.

• The emphasis on strong lay leadership seen in Presbyterian and Disciples churches and the respect and responsibility accorded to lay elders.

• The Presbyterian example of the corporate and collegial manner in which the function of the episcopal office can be carried out by the presbytery.

• The cultural contribution to the English literary heritage of the Episcopalian *Book of Common Prayer*.

• The excellence of musical values upheld in the music of the Episcopal and Lutheran churches.

• The witness of the peace churches—Quaker, Brethren, and Mennonite—in opposing war and taking the Christian role of peacemaker seriously, their history of conscientious objection, and their present concern with simple life-styles that use less of the world's resources.

• The unflagging leadership of the United Church of Christ in controversial social issues.

• The emphasis of various congregational-polity churches on the importance of the local church as the locus of Christian community.

• The Mormons' insistence on the importance of the family unit.

• The centrality of the Eucharist for Episcopalians, Lutherans, and Roman Catholics—a focus that teaches United Methodists much about the meaning of this act.

• The sense of order and accountability in Presbyterian structures; the Presbyterians' concern with parliamentary order.

• The Episcopal Church's role as a bridge between Protestants and Catholics.

United Methodists' self-image as an open and ecumenical people would seem to bode well for the future. The denomination needs, however, to seriously consider the criticisms of those who suggest that the reality does not always agree with the image; that the church often manifests unecumenical attitudes. The observation that United Methodism's size breeds a sense of self-sufficiency raises obvious implications about motivations. If United Methodism sees itself as an integral part of a broader Christian community, then it will be concerned not only for its own needs, but also for the smaller, less affluent denominations which could benefit greatly from the resources United Methodism could bring to any ecumenical endeavor. Of course, it would be unfortunate if that concern were manifested in a condescending Lady Bountiful manner—the haves extending charity to the have-nots. As one can see from the listing of attributes of other denominations, even the smallest of church bodies brings gifts to the ecumenical enterprise. For example, this large denomination could learn much from the small Mennonite Church about living out a commitment to peace.

United Methodism's size and affluence have enabled it to participate in an "easy" ecumenism: It is always able to cooperate in a venture undertaken by a congenial mainline congregation. A more difficult ecumenism for the 1980s may entail struggling with the quest for Christian unity on two other fronts: (a) the Roman Catholic Church, which under the leadership of Pope John Paul II seems to have taken a step backward from post-Vatican II openness; and (b) a growing third force, the burgeoning conservative evangelical wing of Protestantism. Evangelicalism is not at all a monolithic entity, but varies enormously in its receptivity to ecumenical overtures. These tasks will present a major challenge to United Methodism's ecumenical self-image.

CHAPTER 4

The Impact of Place

There is one pitfall when one attempts to generalize about ecumenical attitudes and behavior—in any town or city, reactions are the result of a complex brew of ingredients: the particular denominations and their relative numbers, other cultural factors, strong leaders, geography. As more than one observer notes, United Methodists tend to be theological and cultural chameleons, influenced by the context in which they live out their faith.

In parts of the South where Southern Baptists are the dominant influence, observers note that, especially in rural areas, United Methodist churches "try to out-Baptist the Baptists" with gospel singing, evangelistic preaching, and conservative theology. A district superintendent reports that Baptist tradition is so influential that "you find some Methodists in the rural churches who don't want to baptize babies." Conversely, some churches "stand over against" the Baptists, declaring more assertively a distinctive Methodist identity. A South Carolina pastor recalls, "I used to have a youth group that I nicknamed the post-Baptist therapy group, because I don't care what we discussed, somehow the conversation always got around to stories about growing up in a Baptist church somewhere."

In Texas, United Methodists tend to use the word *preacher* rather consistently in place of *pastor, minister, clergyman,* or *clergywoman.* This suggests that in that part of the country, preaching the Word is widely regarded as the central act of worship, and possibly the most important thing the minister does. Note also that the clergywoman is not merely a *preacher*, but almost invariably a *lady* preacher—perhaps reflecting the fact that ordination of women is less common in the Southwest than in some other parts of the country.

Some southern white preaching tends to resemble black preaching—dramatic, emotion-charged, colorful. One could hypothesize that southern white United Methodists have been influenced by the black church, by Baptist preaching, or simply by the whole southern oratorical tradition.

Some southern United Methodists find that Southern Baptists are becoming more open to ecumenical cooperation than they were several years ago, and the Methodists seem excited by this development. The cooperative Southern Baptists generally are those who are more socially and theologically liberal. But since in some parts of the South *liberal* is a fighting word, the left-of-center folk are careful to characterize their stance as *moderate* or *progressive*.

Adult Sunday schools are stronger in the South—possibly another reflection of Baptist influence. In some parts of the country, however, "church school is for children." In the Midwest, one finds more churches where worship and church school go on simultaneously—a custom which keeps the children out of worship, along with their teachers, and discourages the formation of adult church school classes.

A United Methodist bishop who works in a large Catholic-dominated city relates that bishops, of whatever denomination, are regarded there as "a big deal" more than in areas where he had served previously. Also, United Methodists in that city tend to give more centrality to Communion, celebrating it much more frequently. "I've been asked to administer Communion three or four times a week since I've been here."

Conversely, in parts of the country where frontier circuit riders once made their rounds, the once-a-quarter custom for Communion prevails in local churches. That was about as often as some circuit riders could get to every church on their charge.

A Boston resident finds United Methodists there adopting an apologetic style, feeling numerically inferior, not a part of the city's cultural mainstream. Ecumenism in Massachusetts tends to be "all us Protestants together."

In the far West, United Methodists say that the influence of secularity is a dominant force. But ecumenism seems healthier, perhaps, in a climate where "you know you're going to have to band together to have any impact at all."

United Methodists are very much aware of the burgeoning growth of evangelical churches, as well as the presence of a variety of sects. A glance at the advertisements on the religion page of the Saturday *Los Angeles Times* reveals an amazing proliferation of Christian and non-Christian bodies. In California, it is possible to hold some kinds of interreligious dialogue that could not take place in parts of the country where one never meets a Buddhist, a Sikh, or a Muslim.

An easterner who now lives in Southern California believes that "out here, nobody is quite as strongly what they were back East. When they leave and come out here, they're getting rid of some of the roots. That they are Methodist is an act of nostalgia for childhood days back East. It has to do more with memory than with any special affection for United Methodist polity."

In a suburb of San Francisco, where the church is beset by secularism on one side and a growing fundamentalism on the other, a laywoman says, "United Methodists feel a strong sense of needing to maintain a classic Christian stance, without going to an extreme in either direction."

In Arizona and Nevada, there are areas of expansion with many new people moving in: "The churches are starting afresh and anew, with tremendous growth and enthusiasm."

In Nevada (as in Utah), United Methodists are much aware of the overwhelming Mormon presence, and one result is a greater awareness of the importance of the family. But secularity is as great, or even greater an influence. Despite historic Methodist positions on alcohol and gambling, the churches know that many of their members are employed in bars or in gambling establishments and that people in these "sinful" businesses need the ministry of the church. Because of the Mormon strength and identity and the HAPPINESS IS MORMONISM bumper stickers, United Methodists tend to be more aggressive in asserting their own distinctive identity. Ecumenism in both Nevada and Utah is apt to mean "everybody else except the Mormons getting together."

The Methodist/Evangelical United Brethren (EUB) merger was experienced differently in various parts of the country. The strength of former EUBs in a locality is quickly evident in the tendency of church people either to continue to use the term *Methodist* or to be careful to say *United* Methodist. A clergywoman who formerly worked in Maryland says, "The former EUBs would jump on you there if you didn't say *United.*" A district superintendent in Texas, where there are few EUBs, says that many people in his area resented the name change: "You'll see many signs on churches that indicate that they still haven't changed." Although areas such as Ohio, Wisconsin, and Pennsylvania had to make more adjustments, which inevitably involved a certain amount of pain and conflict, feelings about the merger in strong EUB country tend now to be very positive.

Knowing the cost in time and energy of making union work, some former Methodists and EUBs would not want to go through another such process any time soon. For former EUBs, says one Wisconsinite, "that hurt is still a running sore—especially for the older ones." Some speak wistfully of the gifts they brought to the union that were rejected—term episcopacy, elected superintendents. Even so, former EUBs believe that certain of their valuable attributes have been kept: a needed pietism and an evangelical fervor, for example. The present local church structure, with both a programmatic *and* a policymaking board, was a gift of the EUBs. Still, some former

EUBs feel they have not "melted" into United Methodism, but have been "swallowed up."

A few other random examples of geographical differences in attitudes toward ecumenism may be worth mentioning. The isolation felt by those in underpopulated rural areas has its effect on United Methodists. In rural New England, a laywoman speaks of feeling out of community and cut off from the denomination as a whole. In such a situation, local ecumenical ties may assume greater importance. In rural South Dakota, most churches are small, and "there's no way they can reach out in mission by themselves." Therefore, there are more cooperative efforts. "The pace is slower here," says a pastor. "There's more time to interact, and you can learn to know your neighbor."

In Wisconsin, a pastor suggests that the Lutheran influence prompts more United Methodists to wear clerical collars for their hospital calls and other pastoral work. The Lutheran presence there is also instrumental in the United Methodist emphasis on thorough confirmation class training (up to two years); the decisions to "do it at the same age the Lutherans do it" and to use "white confirmation robes for our kids" were results of Lutheran influence.

In Iowa, United Methodists are the most numerous of any religious group, and it is therefore more difficult for them to be innovative and prophetic, says an observer, simply because there is such a large overlap between the church membership and the population as a whole. "It's hard to be a leader when you have that many constituents."

Just as the Snowbelt and Sunbelt interests are influential in national politics and in voting patterns in the United States Congress, so regional differences show up in the workings of The United Methodist Church. One can clearly discern, for example, strong regional differences in the perceptions of the power of the bishop, the workings of the itineracy, and the use of the consultation process in appointment making. One can see regional differences at work in a General Conference plenary debate, where southern parliamentary virtuosity is apt to dominate the proceedings. Less easy to discern, perhaps, is the way regional differences may affect the ecumenical enterprise as a whole. One could surmise that the Snowbelt regions of United Methodism (North Central and Northeast jurisdictions), which are experiencing more directly the effects of economic recession, rising energy costs, and the decline of older cities, may see more clearly that sharing resources among denominations, or even uniting structurally, could be of benefit. The more prosperous Sunbelt regions (especially Southeast and South Central jurisdictions), feeling the pinch less, are not so inclined to see the practical value of such moves. In any case, the impact of geography on United Methodists is a factor that should not be overlooked by the denomination as it sketches out scenarios for an ecumenical future.

CHAPTER 5

Is Church Union Necessary?

In one of the documents of the Consultation on Church Union, Gerald Moede, the organization's general secretary, speaks of the hope that denominations will reach agreement and take action to hasten the day when, in the words of John Wesley, "Names and sects and parties fall; Thou, O Christ, art all in all."

A small but enthusiastic minority of United Methodists echo that hope. They see the "names and sects and parties" of American denominationalism as signifying "the scandal of disunity" of Christ's Church, and they look forward to the consummation of an organic church union of which United Methodism will be a part.

The large majority of United Methodists, however, do not believe that "Christian unity" necessarily requires "church union." They are entirely comfortable with the idea that America denominations can retain their structural separateness while growing closer together in theological understanding and cooperating more closely in mission.

The Consultation on Church Union came into being in 1962, as four denominations working toward organic church unity in the form of a Church of Christ Uniting. The consultation, familiarly known as COCU, today has ten member denominations (The United Methodist Church, the African Methodist Episcopal Church, the African Methodist Episcopal Zion Church, the Christian Church [Disciples of Christ], the Christian Methodist Episcopal Church, The Episcopal Church, the National Council of Community

Churches, the Presbyterian Church in the United States, the United Church of Christ, and The United Presbyterian Church in the U.S.A.).

Back in 1970, the consultation sent *A Plan of Union* to the denominations for their study. The responses to that document indicated that there was considerable agreement among the churches on matters of faith, worship, and ministry. But the specifications for a united church structure were judged to be premature, and COCU's plan went back for additional work.

However, since that setback to momentum and morale, the consultation has continued to progress in incremental steps. As ecumenists frequently point out, major church union efforts of the scope of COCU—that is, combining a number of denominations—have usually taken forty or more years to bring to fruition. The matter of institutional structures still is perhaps the most difficult problem to be overcome.

In asking United Methodists across the country about their views on COCU, one finds a few who are genuinely enthusiastic. But among the laity, most are only dimly aware of the consultation and its work. Many who have heard the acronym COCU are uncertain what the initials stand for.

But laity, though most of them are uninformed about COCU, often tend to be more open than clergy to the idea of union. Lay people seem to feel a sense of oneness with fellow Christians and see fewer reasons why denominations should be separate. A laywoman at a Week of Christian Unity observance declares, "We're already united, whether we know it or not." This is a commonly expressed sentiment, but when the person who utters it is pressed to say more, it turns out to mean one of two things: (a) "We are one in spirit; therefore it doesn't make sense for us to remain separated by denominational boundaries; the churches should get together structurally"; or (b) "Since we already have spiritual unity anyway, we don't *need* structural unity, and besides, it would be impractical to get rid of our separate denominations."

The laity does not view COCU as a very controversial organization, or as a very potent one. Little information about it filters down to the person in the pew. Many local pastors acknowledge their own failure to educate the laity about COCU or even to transmit information about its progress; it is simply not taken very seriously by most United Methodists. It is the target of small jokes, and it is widely thought of (when it is thought of at all) as a sideline operation run by the professional ecumenists, the theologians, the professors, and the bureaucrats. It is thought to have little relevance for the local church. The responses of many unenthusiastic local church pastors are strikingly similar.

"COCU is kind of a big yawn."

"Nobody has any enthusiasm for COCU anymore except the Disciples of Christ."

"On paper, I hear United Methodism continuing to talk about COCU. But it's dead in terms of the congregations in Florida. It doesn't even exist. Over the past ten years, my observation is that the idea of merger has withered and withered."

A theology professor says that the question of the health of COCU depends upon one's perspective. From the local church level, it may look dead or dying, but "if you're at the meetings, you get a strong sense that these people are there as official representatives of their denominations, and they are serious, and they mean business, and they have some optimism about achievement. I think that's genuine—often to the surprise of people who take part."

Resistance to (or apathy about) COCU is explained in several ways:

1. United Methodists do not want to lose denominational distinctiveness.

2. People see the merging of institutional structures as impractical. It would be so time consuming and difficult that it would take needed energies away from the primary mission of the church.

3. People simply have lost interest because of the slowness of the process.

4. People see other better ways to achieve their Christian unity aims.

Interestingly, it is often the pastors who came to United Methodism from other traditions who can most clearly articulate the qualities in United Methodism that they treasure and that they would fear losing in a union. A pastor who was raised a Southern Baptist says that he could never preach in a Southern Baptist church because he cannot accept some of their doctrinal positions. "Also," he adds, "I cherish the United Methodist pastoral appointment system. It makes for more graceful transitions, without the trauma of firing a pastor, and it ensures employment for the clergy."

Another pastor complains that the denomination is moving toward congregationalism, as opposed to connectionalism. He feels that when the cabinet consults with the pastor and the Pastor-Parish Relations Committee before making an appointment, the committee "can veto the power to make appointments." He adds that while the congregational system may work for fundamentalists and evangelicals, a more liberal denomination needs "good strong bishops."

For some, the prospect of church union raises the troubling specter of a loss of identity. A clergywoman says, "I sense there's going to be a real struggle if COCU ever comes about, if it reaches a point where we're not talking about United Methodist or UCC or Presbyterian. It has to do with a person's identity and who they understand themselves to be. If we're called Church of Christ Uniting rather than United Methodist, then that says something about who I am and who I was and who I'm not any longer."

One pastor voices his objections to the idea of merger with other denominations: "I really believe God has different ministries for us, that he called denominations into existence to emphasize something that was being neglected. One denomination emphasizes the Sacraments, another the Bible, others the sovereignty of God or personal faith experience."

But resistance to COCU is, in the minds of some, a resistance to change: "Everything else in the culture is changing so rapidly that people look to the church as the one place that doesn't change too much. The idea is, if the good ol' Methodist and Presbyterian churches were good enough for Paul and Silas, they're good enough for us."

Much of the objection to COCU seems to be based on the fear that it would produce a monolithic church that would not encourage diversity. Says a California clergyman, "It's an attempt to water down everybody's theology and commitments and would create a superchurch. The church does not need to be another General Motors hierarchy. We've already got too much of that in the church."

A church-union advocate offers this observation: "I personally do not think that the conception of cooperation is adequate to meet the needs of our current situation. I don't think the superchurch that people are worried about is going to happen." He points out that, though the Roman Catholic Church is the largest Christian body in the world, "I can go to two different Roman Catholic churches in this town, and their services will be as different as the Baptist and Methodist may be. They have unity with diversity."

Many believe that the real opposition to COCU is from pastors, bureaucrats, and middle-judicatory officials who tend to be more familiar with and concerned about intricacies of structure. To many lay people, for whom *church* means the local church, the questions of altering mid-level structural machinery are unimportant, and they see little to separate one denomination from another.

Persons in The United Methodist Church who characterize themselves as evangelicals criticize the emphasis on union with so-called liberal denominations; they themselves would be far more enthusiastic about union with more conservative bodies which have Wesleyan roots—Wesleyans, Free Methodists, Nazarenes.

Interviewees typically commented on the slowness of the COCU process. A layman in Massachusetts says, "Most of us are not likely to invest significant amounts of time and energy planting trees that are going to bear fruit in our children's lifetime. We want to pluck the fruit from the trees that are already planted."

Because of that slowness, many who once had hopes for COCU have become dispirited. A seminary staff member speaks of a colleague "who taught a course in ecumenics around 1960, at which time he was talking about how terrific COCU would be, and by 1980 we would be one church united. Here we are, twenty years later, and we're nowhere near that."

Many ecumenists believe another route may better accomplish unity aims. An executive of a metropolitan council of churches who thinks COCU's theology is "great," says, "We have to come together—not worrying about organizational matters, but beginning to do mission together. I find that if you get together in mission, pretty soon people want to get closer together."

Many who do not envision the establishment of a structural union do appreciate COCU's efforts. Perhaps it is the *process* of theological conversation rather than its end that is important. The consultation is regarded as having made some real accomplishments, such as redefining mission and helping many to understand the meaning of baptism—to understand that membership in the Body of Christ is beyond denominational affiliation.

One man interviewed says that COCU has not been a "priority item" for the church and thus has not received enough exposure in terms of publicity. "If church union were a quadrennial emphasis, the average person's knowldge of COCU would increase almost unbelievably. That's not saying which way they'd go—for or against—but you would not run into the raised eyebrow and the questioning inflection in the voice."

It is almost universally agreed that COCU's 1970 *Plan of Union* was a failure. There now seems to be a concern to reassure people that organic union does *not* mean structural uniformity at all levels and that there can be unity with diversity. What "unity with diversity" would mean is not entirely in focus right now, but as one leader observes, "Ambiguity is right at the heart of the unity movement. We've been saying till we're blue in the face—some of us for thirty years—that we're not trying to obliterate denominational practices and traditions and ways of worship and theology. Nor do we have any intention of obliterating ethnic identities." Still, many wonder whether sufficient diversity can be built into a unity scheme.

Persons involved in COCU's conversations find themselves serving as interpreters in local areas. "My experience has shown me," says one, "that I have to show people what's in it for them. I hear a lot of approval, theoretically, until it comes to details of how it would work. As long as it's mutual recognition of members and ministers, or finding ways to share some of our buildings, people approve. But the thought of having one church, with one name, one group of leaders. . . . "

A pastor talks about the difference between the theological and the practical in attitudes toward union: "If people buy church union, they'll buy it on a pragmatic basis. Most people are not that concerned about theology—or they're concerned about theology in a secondary sense: Is it biblical? Is it right to do this? Is it OK with God for us to get together? I think their answer is almost intuitively Yes." He goes on to say that the mechanics are difficult. "But people will be much more apt to accept unity if you show them why and how it will work."

What implications can be drawn about the future of church union efforts, from the enthusiasm of the few and the unenthusiasm of the many?

First of all, United Methodists, activists that they are, have a characteristic impatience to accomplish a task quickly and move on to the next. Since the denomination marks time by the quadrennium, it is difficult to sustain interest in one cause or issue or task much longer than that. But church union cannot be a casual topic. It is, by its nature, a lengthy process, calling for great patience and diligence. It is a race for long-distance runners, not for sprinters. And although COCU is put on the "back burner" at times, as far as public attention is concerned, people need to understand that the job is one that may not be finished during the lifetime of some of the consultation's founders. But that fact is not in itself a valid argument against it.

Also, one should not make the automatic assumption that, if ecumenists keep plugging away at the task for thirty years or so, the Church of Christ Uniting will inevitably come into being. The steps COCU has taken so far have easily won General Conference approval, usually without even generating much debate. And steps such as "the mutual recognition of members" have been approved by all ten of COCU's member bodies.

These early stages have not demanded significant changes or sacrifices or any relinquishing of what one ecumenist calls "cherished impediments to unity." No one has had to bite the bullet. But as COCU begins to deal more closely with matters of structure and polity, making proposals that affect the functioning of annual conferences and general agencies, the denomination will give closer scrutiny to the implications of continued United Methodist involvement. It is not inconceivable that the church, at some point, could say No to continuing this lengthy negotiation.

As long as folks are yawning, the ecumenists can continue "their little game," and COCU will present no threat to the status quo. But a No is likely if United Methodists suddenly find their identity and tradition and valued elements of polity and style about to be changed. If organic union is seen to loom as a live option, calling for immediate changes in denominational machinery, then one may expect a lively controversy.

"Ecumenical fatigue" and "restructure shock" must also be taken into account. Some parts of United Methodism are still dealing with the "healing process" in the aftermath of the Methodist/EUB merger. The church is also still recovering from the various restructurings of general agencies. Recalling the time and energy spent on these adjustments (and in some cases the hurt, conflict, and loss), church leaders will want to be confident that the gains are worth the costs in any subsequent overhauling for the sake of Christian unity.

A financial crisis caused by rampant inflation or other economic factors could lead The United Methodist Church and other denominations to see COCU efforts as expendable. Rather than kill it outright, however, they might just let it starve for funds. These same financial factors could, on the other hand, accentuate the need for closer structural collaboration between denominations. (A more general discussion of economic factors can be found in chapter 9). But the process of discovering how we can work more creatively in collaboration with our counterparts in other COCU churches need not wait until action is necessitated by economic disaster.

There needs to be much more dialogue at all levels between those who believe that God is calling the churches to work toward organic union, and those who believe just as strongly that unity is to be found instead in cooperation, understanding, and "spiritual oneness." These differences need to be honestly faced and resolved before the denomination can wholeheartedly establish an ecumenical direction for its third century. Right now, those who hold these two opposing views are not really listening to each other.

Some unsettling truths about church union must be faced. Even a Church of Christ Uniting is only a token beginning toward the unity of Christ's Church. The ten denominations in the consultation represent only a tiny fraction of Christendom. Moreover, even as COCU members are articulating their commitment to Christian unity, there are opposing forces of fracture, dissension, and schism that continue to rock several of the denominations. When one looks at the recent history of Protestantism in the United States, for example, one can count more church schisms than unions. Like the mythical Sisyphus, toiling up to the mountaintop with a boulder only to see it roll down again, ecumenists are engaged in what must seem a never-to-be-completed effort.

These next years may well be ones in which The United Methodist Church struggles to arrive at some consensus as to whether organic union is the necessary and faithful response to Christ's prayer "that they may all be one."

CHAPTER 6

Local Vitality: What's the Payoff?

The most lively things happening ecumenically, say many United Methodists, are at the local level and are centered on issues. This does not mean that there is no vitality at other levels. Indeed, United Methodists who are actually involved in world, national, or state level ecumenical bodies have a great deal of enthusiasm for and commitment to the work of those bodies. A minister in Washington, D.C., cautions, "It's a healthy reality that there's more interest in local ecumenism. But that shouldn't be used to discredit other levels." But pastors and laity at the grass-roots level, though they may acknowledge the importance of ecumenism beyond the local, say that it seldom directly touches their lives or their local church. Local ecumenical cooperation generates far more interest, simply because it is more visible and closer to home. Local people can see the effects; they can participate in decision making and action.

Virtually every pastor believes his or her first priority is the local congregation. Pastors talk about heavy demands on their time and say that they are not inclined to spend it on ecumenical efforts unless those efforts benefit the local church or community. Lay people add that a congregation is not apt to become involved unless their pastor advocates it. "Generally, if the pastor doesn't want something to happen, it doesn't happen." As one pastor puts it, when considering time and work involvements, *"What's the payoff?* There's an immediate payoff in local cooperation. It does something for the community. It's a *visible* kind of ecumenism." Other pastors make essentially the same point, though they may express it less bluntly.

What are some of these payoffs? What are the needs that prompt ecumenical behavior at the local level? Let us look at a dozen different motives for ecumenism, bearing in mind that most will have the characteristic element of practicality and that some will apply to ecumenism beyond the local level.

1. *The Need for Friendship and Mutual Support.* A great proportion of local ecumenical involvements begin with relationships between pastors. Grass-roots coalitions begin, says one observer, "when clergy in three or four neighborhood churches get to know and trust one another and develop a commitment of person to person." Many pastors remark on the pressures of their profession, the morale problems, the need for networks of support from other persons who understand their situation. Pastors tend to form friendships and support groups with other clergy rather than with laity. There seems to be almost a taboo against forming extremely close friendships with lay people, especially those in their own congregations. This tendency may be related to the pastor's sense of being only a temporary sojourner in the community, one who will before too long be appointed to serve a church in another locality.

Many United Methodist pastors, for reasons related to the connectional system, appear to confide less in their denominational colleagues than they do in ministers of other denominations. For many, there is an element of competition within their denomination. "It's a helpful relief to be able to talk to another pastor about some of your worries and frustrations," says one clergyman, "and it's good that we can pray together. Pastors need to be friends. If you really say what you're thinking to other United Methodists, you feel that it will get back to the superintendent or to the bishop. You feel more free with ministers from other denominations." A seminary specialist in clinical pastoral education told one pastor, "Never rely on other United Methodist pastors for your support. I've started a dozen clergy groups, and they do great until about April, and then when appointment making starts, the thing falls apart. You may not like it, but you're in competition with those people, and you measure yourself against them, and you resent it when they do better."

Particularly in a small-town or country situation where there may be only one United Methodist pastor in the area, he or she is likely to form friendships with clergy of other denominations. "Loneliness brings about a lot of cooperation."

Women clergy seem to feel particularly isolated and in need of support networks. Still a very small minority, most face the pressure of being the first woman or the only woman in many situations and must prove themselves to male colleagues as well as to the laity. Ecumenical support groups of women clergy are fairly common and generally provide fellowship and the opportunity to share common concerns.

Similarly, ethnic-minority clergy who may have a sense of isolation in their own denomination often form networks for mutual support with their counterparts in other church bodies.

A southern pastor observes that there may be more sense of unity across denomintional lines with people who share the same visions and commitments, than with United Methodist colleagues one disagrees with.

In most towns of any size, even though there may be very little ecumenical cooperation, there is a formally organized ministerial alliance, which may be merely a "meet-and-eat" group or may have more extensive functions. These groups, besides serving fellowship purposes, are often the launching pads for cooperative service or action, particularly if there is no local council of churches.

2. *The Need for Resources and Intellectual Stimulation.* Some of the ecumenical pastoral support groups provide intellectual refreshment and the exchange of ideas. Many pastors mention the value of participating in regular weekly get-togethers for Bible study and discussion of sermon preparation, using the

ecumenical lectionary. One remarks, "The common lectionary has had tremendous practical cooperative impact. I would never have looked to liturgy as being an organizing source or center for cooperation, but it surely has been that."

Another minister advocates the idea that pastors can be resources for one another and that this reduces the sense of competitiveness: "The threat level goes down if we understand that we each have gifts and that there are things we can learn from other pastors."

3. *The Need to Present a United Front for Effectiveness in Addressing Controversial Issues.* When clergy and laity feel called to take a stand on some controversial issue that does not have the general support of their congregation and community, they know they can "take the heat" better if they have allies and that their statement will carry more weight when it is added to statements from like-minded persons from other church bodies.

Many activists mention crises that were the catalysts for bringing people together for joint action. Sometimes what was envisioned as a temporary emergency coalition grew into a permanent fixture on the local ecumenical scene. Crises of the recent decades—school-desegregation battles, reactions to assassinations, urban riots, open-housing marches, anti-Vietnam protests, draft counseling—provided the immediate impetus for the formation of some coalitions that are still active today. "If the structure is already in place, then you can react more quickly when the emergency arises," says one activist.

4. *The Desire to Benefit the Community with a Project That One Church Cannot Accomplish by Itself.* A St. Louis neighborhood coalition sprang up to combat "redlining" by banks and "blockbusting" by realtors, practices that threatened the stability of the community, and thus that of the churches.

In South Dakota, an ecumenical group raised a question about uranium mining: How would it affect the health of persons in the community?

If only a few members of a congregation would like to

sponsor a refugee family, they may lack the resources of time and money to accomplish the task. But it may be possible to undertake the project if they can find sympathetic persons in other congregations who will join with them.

The hunger issue, which is not just one issue but a whole cluster of related concerns, was often mentioned as an interest that unites liberals and conservatives. However, while world hunger is a strong concern, there is more likely to be an effort to feed persons in one's own locality. Many communties have ecumenically sponsored Meals on Wheels projects to deliver hot meals to elderly and homebound persons, and many have emergency food pantries. Cooperative ministries to transients and indigents often grow from a practical need for coordination, when it is discovered that the same persons are making the rounds, voicing the same plea at half a dozen neighborhood churches. When the churches work together, all persons in need of help can be referred to a central location and duplication of services can be avoided.

Sometimes United Methodists will act ecumenically by helping fund a project sponsored by another denomination. In one area, United Methodists gave money to the Lutheran Social Service Center: "We could not afford an agency with the quality staff they had." In other cases, a United Methodist-sponsored project—for example, a neighborhood center—will draw the support of other congregations who see the need for such a ministry but lack the resources to sponsor one of their own.

There is an amazing variety of local ecumenical ministries of service and action to meet human need:

• A coalition of mainliners, storefront preachers, and Pentecostals initiates a ministry to Spanish-speaking people.

• A clergy association or a council of churches establishes an industrial chaplaincy or maintains a chaplaincy in a jail, hospital, juvenile center, or at a campsite.

• With United Methodists taking the lead, several churches

sponsor a recycling project, using one church as the headquarters for collecting cans, bottles, and papers.

• Local church leaders, both liberal and conservative, raise funds to build a chapel on the grounds of a state school for persons with mental handicaps, since state law forbids a chapel to be built with state funds.

• A metropolitan council of churches supports civil rights for homosexuals, in opposition to the conservative Christians' antigay crusade.

• A consortium of ten neighborhood churches starts a holistic health center.

• Mainline churches fund and staff a needed inner-city theological training center for storefront Baptist and Pentecostal pastors.

• A neighborhood coalition of pastors tries to stop an old residential hotel in their neighborhood from "going condo" and evicting the elderly residents who cannot afford to buy the apartments.

• United Methodists lead an ecumenical coalition in establishing a "court of last resort" where people in desperate straits can obtain help until more permanent income becomes available.

• A council of churches forms a nonprofit corporation to build apartments for senior citizens.

• A ministerial fellowship coordinates the daily devotions for a local radio station.

• Churches hold a "counter rally" to combat the influence of the Ku Klux Klan—they ring church bells and meet in the daylight hours, "as opposed to the darkness the Klan uses."

Ecumenical cooperation is by no means a monopoly of liberals. Some coalitions attract *only* the more conservative. For example, in any city where the Billy Graham Association (or some other visiting evangelistic association) holds a crusade, an effort is made by the local committee to obtain the backing of a majority of churches. Generally some United Methodists believe the crusade will benefit the community, and they participate. Others regard it as a kind of evangelism that is unlikely to benefit either the community or the local church; these pastors and congregations decline.

Conservatives also are combining efforts in an area of Texas where the sale of liquor is still a matter for dispute. The more conservative pastors engage fully in the fight against legalization, remarking that "this is one of the few things that the Baptists and the Churches of Christ will work with the Methodists on." But some United Methodists and other moderates, and those mainliners whose members are more likely to practice social drinking, issue a more ambiguous statement on the issue.

United Methodists sometimes are among those cooperating in fundamentalist, politically oriented groups such as Moral Majority, though leadership typically comes from conservative evangelical denominations. Such groups also have their own vision of what needs to be done to benefit the community—and that may mean a right-to-life (antiabortion) campaign, the defeat of liberal political candidates, support of capital punishment, or the removal of certain books from public and school library shelves.

5. *The Desire for Some Religious Experience or Sustenance That Is Unavailable from One's Local Church.* In many communities, a lively, unofficial, and largely lay-led ecumenism operates outside denominational sponsorship. In some cases, the focus is on charismatic experience, and the vehicle is a network of prayer groups that meet in homes. Much of United Methodism regards "speaking in tongues" as a divisive, church-splitting practice. Therefore, rather than trying to "do their thing" within church-sponsored prayer and Bible study groups, charismatic United Methodists often stay in the closet at their local church (though they continue to be active members for a variety of reasons). They pursue the charismatic experience in unofficial groups with like-minded Christians from a variety of other churches (often including Roman Catholic).

Similarly, nondenominational women's groups—Women

Aglow, Christian women's clubs, and the like—seem to supply a dimension not available either from United Methodist Women or from more liberal/activist ecumenical groups such as Church Women United. And some find a feeling of oneness that transcends denominationalism. These groups may be social, with luncheons and speakers, or they may be more religiously oriented, but they fill the need for fellowship and friendship. The women they appeal to apparently have a theology and life-style more in common with one another than with women in their own denomination's structures.

6. *The Desire to Serve the Needs of the Local Congregation Whose Resources Are Insufficient.* "Smaller churches and their ministers," says a seminary professor, "involve themselves in ecumenical activities more than the larger ones, partly because a church has to be a certain size before it can adequately utilize the resources of the denomination, many of which are designed for larger churches." In the large church, more personnel and more financial resources are available. Cooperation among smaller churches may result in joint vacation church schools; a shared year-round Christian education program; combined choral groups, which offer the community a more impressive performance; cooperative lay leadership training, with groups from several churches, including Presbyterians, Episcopalians, and Disciples; regional ecumenical conferences on religion, art, and architecture to help in planning building programs. Two small neighboring churches in the Snowbelt (with high heating bills) may agree to meet in the same building during winter months—either scheduling services at different hours or worshiping together. Economic necessity may lead two or more struggling congregations into an even closer working relationship—a yoked parish arrangement, where a pastor of one denomination serves more than one church. This is similar to the "circuit" arrangement, except that one or more of the churches is non-United Methodist.

7. *Mixed Motives: Generosity, Profit, and "We Need Each Other."* Congregations tend to need their own "turf" and are reluctant

to share their property with another congregation. Yet there are many instances in which one congregation pays a modest rental to another congregation, in order to hold worship and other activities in their building. This arrangement benefits both. Often the congregations are very different in denomination, language, and culture. There is an element of practical economics in the recognition that the host congregation can use the rental fee to help meet expenses and that otherwise the building would be standing empty and unused for most of the week. And there is an element of "we need each other"—one congregation needs a roof over its head; the other needs not only the rent money but the opportunity to get beyond parochialism, to be exposed to persons outside their small circle.

Some examples of this kind of "ecumenism" include a United Methodist church which has torn down its own building to erect a new one on the same site and has moved in with the Congregational church down the street, "the nearest and most friendly congregation," for the duration; a congregation of the Metropolitan Community Church (ministering to homosexuals) which meets in a United Methodist church; and a Jewish congregation which meets in a United Methodist sanctuary until its own temple is built.

There are also many instances of black or Spanish-speaking Pentecostal or evangelical congregations meeting in United Methodist churches. Sometimes there are tensions over differences in life-styles and housekeeping matters, but usually the congregations lead separate lives. Most such arrangements are temporary, since the "guest" congregation is usually a new and struggling church, looking forward to the day when it can afford its own building. The ecumenical limitations of such arrangements are obvious. Since one congregation is landlord and the other tenant, there can never be a sense of meeting as equal partners. One often feels like an intruder; the other senses that its building has been misused. "Those people didn't leave our kitchen clean. And their kids' shoes made scuff marks on the newly waxed hall floors."

What about two churches sharing a building for the long term, in an equal partnership? Says one church-sharer, "They aren't doing it yet because of pride, because of turf, because the OPEC oil increases haven't hit them that severely yet. But they will. And if we ever have local governments taxing church properties, there's going to be a lot of these congregations with these neo-Gothic monuments that will want to combine with other congregations in an adaptable building, and forget their turf. I would hail that day, because it exemplifies a Christian concept of stewardship."

8. *Minimal Motives: A Matter of Practicing Common Courtesy, of Fulfilling Expectations, of Meeting Obligations, of Maintaining Relations.* Sad to say, ecumenical worship services often fall into one or the other of the above categories, and so do some of the occasions when church leaders sign their names to a common statement on some social issue. There is, occasionally, the feeling that "we ought to" when the time comes for displaying ecumenical effort. One comment from an interviewee reflects this motivation: "Sometimes, unfortunately, our main motivation is to *show* how ecumenical we are. It's like saying, 'Hey, let's do something together for the sake of saying we did it together.' " Another person states, "Our Catholic, Protestant, and Jewish communities are amicable. We get together on all the right occasions. It's a matter of liturgical courtesy, a ceremonial ecumenism, more born out of a tradition of reserved politeness than from any imperative to be in community, or any real persuasion that we're working toward a common stand on significant social issues."

9. *A Taken-for-Granted Openness.* United Methodists have a natural openness that is an integral part of their heritage. Some of the signs of this receptiveness are not much reflected upon, and most would not think of them as ecumenical. For example, a local church's willingness to hire a non-United Methodist choir director, organist, church secretary, or janitor

viewed as a move to increase Christian unity. There are even some instances of openness to using non-United Methodists in professional ordained-ministry functions.

There is usually no problem when a visiting pastor or priest performs a wedding ceremony in a local church. In fact, it is usual for the officiating to be shared with the host pastor. There is also an openness to performing marriages for persons of other denominations. Some pastors say they most frequently deal with ecumenism at this level. "Almost every United Methodist here seems to be marrying someone of a different denomination. In marriage counseling, I help them to identify who they are and how they are going to act out their faith corporately. I help them and their families come to an understanding of ecumenism." In Arizona not long ago, a United Methodist church offered its building for the 150th anniversary celebration of a local Catholic hospital. On the one hand, it was a good public relations gesture and a practical solution, since the sanctuary is the largest in town. On another level, it was the working of that automatic openness. It would not have occurred to the United Methodists to say No to an opportunity to give what was needed by another group of Christians in that situation.

10. *A Yearning to Act Out the Gift of Unity with All Christians.* Despite the frequent presence of more cynical or pragmatic motives, when one talks to many United Methodists, one is drawn to the conclusion that ecumenical activities are often motivated by a genuine yearning toward Christian unity. Depending upon the level of theological sophistication and articulateness of the respondent, this may be expressed in fairly complex language approximating that of ecumenical documents, or more simply, as a hunch that Christians ought to be working, worshiping, and enjoying fellowship together.

As a laywoman expresses it, "All Christians are members of one Body. Other Christians are not the enemy. They're our friends." And a minister voices her vision: "We already are one—the whole family is one—and we just don't know that yet. Ecumenism is discovering what already is."

Several persons expressed the thought that worshiping together grows naturally from the feeling of oneness that comes from working together on critical issues. One ecumenical executive explains: "I recall a few years ago when a couple of our people were in jail for trespassing at Trident [a submarine base] during an antinuclear demonstration. I wrote a letter to the bishops and denominational leaders inviting them to greet these two when they came out of jail after spending ninety days there. The clergy and all the denominational heads marched through town and then had a big worship service in First United Methodist Church. It was a glorious ecumenical experience, but it was around a real event in the life of the church."

"The ecumenical gatherings that have really stirred me," says a conference council director, "have been the ones where I sensed again that we had rediscovered something of the ground on which we stood as common."

The interviewees who conveyed a sense of excitement were, almost without exception, talking about: (a) Protestant-Catholic experiences; (b) Christian-Jewish dialogue; or (c) relations with Southern Baptists and other evangelicals, who a few years ago had seemed less open to ecumenism. But in every case, there is a distance still to be bridged.

11. *A Desire to Be Educated, to Better Understand Other Traditions.* The motive for understanding often underlies the enthusiasm for Christian/Jewish dialogue. The press of world events seems, at least in some localities, to have made people aware of the need to learn more about other world religions, especially Islam. This is more likely to happen in a city where there are considerable numbers of Muslims. "There are some people," says a district superintendent, "who are more interested in this because their consciousness has been raised by the Mideast crisis."

In general, however, interreligious dialogue seems to have a lower priority than ecumenical contacts with other Christians.

12. *Serendipity: The Unmotivated Ecumenical Experience.* Many United Methodists report stumbling into positive personal experiences which they subsequently interpreted as being ecumenical. A teacher in a United Methodist college discovers he has "a Church of Christ lady" in his Bible class and is surprised to find her "very much liberated. If you didn't know she was Church of Christ, you'd almost think she was a United Methodist." Meanwhile, a student studying for the ministry at that same college takes a preaching course at a university of another denomination across town. Expecting members of that church to be "narrow," he finds a surprising commonality: "We both had misconceptions of the other. But I found them open to learning about our church. I found out they preach the Bible just like anybody else does, and they have a love for the Lord and God's Word, just like Christians in other denominations."

Whatever their motives, United Methodists at the local level are engaging in a rich variety of ecumenical activities. However pragmatic or utilitarian United Methodists are in their approach to Christian unity, most of these instances of ecumenical involvement never would happen, were it not for an instinctive affirmative response to the question, Is this what God would have us do?

CHAPTER 7

The Scene at Other Levels

"Local church people don't have a good grasp of ecumenism beyond the local," says an ecumenical executive, "because it doesn't impact their lives."

The National Council of Churches (NCC), founded in 1950, now has 30 member communions; and the World Council of Churches (WCC), organized in 1948, has some 286 member denominations. Both bodies are largely Protestant, but also include some Eastern Orthodox groups. The Roman Catholic Church is not a part of either organization. Perceptions of the work of these agencies are fuzzy, but despite the general lack of knowledge, there is widespread support for both organizations, either on the basis that "we've always done it," or the assumption that a cooperative approach to mission avoids duplication of effort and constitutes "good stewardship."

Where there is an awareness of the NCC's television and broadcast ministries, for instance, or of its work in refugee resettlement or disaster relief, these are appreciated. One pastor says, "We try not to mention the National Council when we raise money for hunger. We do better to speak of churches working together than mentioning the name of an organization that may have a bad reputation in this part of the country."

Some church officials find that they spend a great deal of energy "putting out brushfires" when criticism erupts from a vocal minority. In recent years, the most severe criticism has erupted over certain grants made by the World Council's Program to Combat Racism, seen by some as "supporting terrorism." A black layman believes that the "national anxiety" about the WCC has its roots in white American Protestants' "fear of Third-World consciousness and Third-World leadership in that body." On the other hand, there is support for WCC programs "that would feed the heathen and spread the Word in the traditional missionary modality."

The National Council of Churches has been a target of denunciation recently for misunderstandings over the intent and scope of a project to produce an inclusive language lectionary of Scripture passages as a resource for public worship. The project has been interpreted by some as an effort to "rewrite the Bible to suit the feminists."

A professor who has participated in Faith and Order conversations says, "The stance of the World Council and National Council has been that they speak to denominations and not to the local churches. They provide resources for the national churches to translate down to their own constituency. Some denominations pass these on through publications about the importance of things happening ecumenically; some choose not to. Some of the material is lying on the desks of people who were responsible for passing it on down."

Another professor has the perception that misunderstandings are being corrected and that "after these years of interpretation, there's an appreciation of what's happened." One pastor who has conscientiously taken on the interpretative task says, "I have followed all the assemblies of the World Council and preached some of their pronouncements to my congregation. I've read and marked and digested those and given them to my people in preaching and teaching."

Even if there is not widespread enthusiasm, those who are knowledgeable about the work of these agencies testify that they are vital for the common life of the churches. Still, the lack of interest, the misconceptions, and the blurred images of these councils suggest that more effective interpretation is needed at the local level or that the functions of the WCC and NCC need to be clarified. Perhaps such questions as these need to be asked:

1. Who are the people who need to take responsibility for interpreting the National Council of Churches and World Council of Churches?

2. Can The United Methodist Church's participants in WCC and NCC anticipate the actions or statements that will be controversial, and can they report an accurate version of council actions to the churches before the people learn about them from secular media?

3. Can council interpreters build good working relationships with the secular press, with the result that stories would not be distorted by omission or oversimplification? Can church members be encouraged to read denominational publications for more detailed reports and analyses from a religious perspective?

4. Can the heavy wooden style of ecumenical documents be translated into clear, readable prose? Can dry documents be enlivened with accompanying explanations that will give the average reader better information?

5. Can more personnel be made available to interpret, in person, the work of the WCC and NCC to local churches, districts, and annual conferences?

6. Do United Methodist publications have a responsibility to be advocates for the WCC, the NCC, and United Methodist participation in these bodies? Or should they simply report the facts?

7. How can local church members be made to feel that their voices are heard by NCC and WCC decision makers and that there is adequate accountability which does not ignore grass-roots thinking?

World Methodist Council

A far less controversial worldwide ecumenical body is the World Methodist Council. One also finds little knowledge of or interest in this organization in local United Methodist churches. Some would not even think of it as being an ecumenical body, although it clearly is. It is somewhat analogous to the world confessional bodies of other traditions, such as The Lutheran World Federation, The Baptist World Alliance, the World Alliance of Reformed Churches, and the Anglican Communion.

This council's membership includes autonomous Methodist denominations around the world. Among members in the United States are such denominations with Wesleyan roots as the Wesleyan Church, the Free Methodist, the Primitive Methodist Church, The United Methodist Church, the Christian Methodist Episcopal Church, the African Methodist Episcopal Church, and the African Methodist Episcopal Zion Church. "One of the greatest things the council has done," says one leader, "has been to bring us (United Methodists) into closer relationship with black Methodist bodies." Conservative elements in our denomination appreciate the contact with conservative Wesleyans, for they believe that greater emphasis should be placed on developing ties with these churches, rather than solely with more liberal mainline bodies.

Other respondents mention an appreciation for the World Methodist Council's work in bilateral dialogues with Roman Catholics and Lutherans; for the conferences every five years that provide the opportunity for Methodists from around the world to meet together; for the pastoral exchange program, in which pastors in the United States and other countries (chiefly Britain) exchange pulpits for several months; and for its world evangelism program.

One hears little criticism of the council among United Methodists, but occasionally the charge is leveled that United Methodist decision makers in the council are predominantly male bishops and clergy—that too few women, laity, and minorities are included. Questions are raised, too, as to whether the World Methodist Council is really a necessary organization and whether its purpose and function justify its cost. There is at present no clear consensus within the denomination on the importance of the council as one facet of the church's ecumenical commitment. In the absence of controversy, however, it appears likely that this council, with its relatively low profile, will quietly continue its work, with the assured participation and funding of United Methodists.

Theological Dialogues

From time to time, United Methodists are engaged in theological dialogues with other Christian bodies—for example, with Lutherans and with Roman Catholics. Duly appointed representatives of the denominations, over a period of years, seek to work out common understandings on such subjects as Holy Communion, baptism, and the Holy Spirit. Though the theological fine points discussed in such dialogues may seem esoteric to most church members, the conversations could ultimately result in understandings such as those now prevailing among the ten churches of COCU—agreements that could make possible inter-Communion, as well as the mutual recognition of members and ministers. Such developments would no doubt be welcomed by most United Methodists.

A layman comments, "Beyond what the hierarchy says, my sense is that most Protestants feel reasonably comfortable with most Catholic layfolk. I find the divisions in the Christian community silly and frivolous. I would be absolutely comfortable being 'married' to my sisters and brothers in the Protestant community, and to many in the Catholic community."

One participant in a United Methodist/Roman Catholic dialogue reports that it "involved looking at our history and identifying the common points, as well as looking at how we can move and change. It's sort of like coming through the past to discover things we hadn't previously discovered about ourselves, in the effort to move closer together, to identify those things we share in common, and to celebrate those things. There was frustration, knowing that we shared so much and yet were not able to surface and articulate and identify it openly."

Most church people seem not to be aware that such dialogues are taking place, though the participants attempt to play an interpretive role, "helping people sense the excitement and possibilities in that kind of dialogue."

The Annual Conference Level

The middle judicatory, or annual conference level, is regarded by many of those interviewed as the most troublesome level for ecumenical relationships. Part of the difficulty is that the boundaries and structures of United Methodist conferences and districts do not match the middle-governing units of other denominations—presbyteries, dioceses, synods, classes, associations, and so on.

The middle judicatory is the level at which agreements are worked out between denominations on strategies for yoked parishes and other ecumenical ministries. "It's a hassle," says a Missouri respondent, "because of the different polities and the different ways of calling ministers. I don't mean it's insurmountable, but in our annual conferences we treat it as though it were. We don't know what to do about that middle stratum. That's where the really nitty-gritty matters of salary, pensions, property, and benevolences are worked out."

Bishops, cabinets, and conference council staffs are seen as having a key linking and interpretive role between the general church and the local church. As one superintendent expresses her view of that function, "The cabinet's role is to be the link not only within United Methodism, but within the Christian faith among denominations. How that gets done probably varies with the individual. Using the ecumenical lectionary is a concrete way to help people see our relationship to other churches."

A conference council director finds that his interpretive role includes disseminating literature from world and national councils. Then "once or twice a year something hits the public press, and you make some calls to the people who can give you firsthand information, and you put together a response." Interpretation is also a routine task, since the staff person goes out to work with individual congregations.

A southern pastor thinks that leadership at the annual conference level is "the most conservative when it comes to the ecumenical movement. This level has the greatest stake in keeping things exactly as they are." A superintendent agrees: "There's a real gap at district level. We're so pressured to push our own program that I have very little opportunity to be involved with other projects."

One ecumenical theologian sees a "lukewarm tokenism" in the way annual conferences put ecumenical affairs on the agenda. "*The Discipline* requires conferences to have some kind of structure for ecumenical affairs. But very often, persons are appointed to these without a clear mandate or experience in doing it." He also finds a "malaise" in councils of churches at the metropolitan and state level. "Some of those which ten or fifteen years ago were humming along quite well have fallen on hard times. There has been a retraction of financial support."

The demise of some metropolitan ecumenical agencies and the loss of vitality on the part of others in the 1960s and 1970s is a development that angers and saddens committed ecumenists. "I find it very discouraging," says a laywoman about her city's failed ecumenical bodies. "My own gut feeling is that the lack of grass-roots participation was part of the reason for demise, along with the disenchantment after the upheavals of the 1960s. The emphasis on the local church was wiped out, and that was a mistake, strategy-wise." A key development in metropolitan and state ecumenical bodies in recent decades has been the shift from councils of churches with local church support, to judicatory-based structures. The restructuring of these mid-level ecumenical agencies was in some cases aimed at obtaining a more secure base for funding, so that the agencies could be bolder in their witness; in other situations, the purpose was to draw in Orthodox, Roman Catholic, and Lutheran groups that previously had not been members.

Opinions differ as to whether various restructures have rendered the agencies healthier or more precarious.

Where state ecumenical agencies or coalitions are lively, they are often involved in lobbying efforts in the state legislature. A Texan active in state-level activity recalls a church/state issue relating to the licensing of children's homes which brought together Southern Baptist, Church of Christ, Roman Catholic, and Greek Orthodox, as well as the mainline denominations. "It was the first time," he says, "I've ever seen all these groups work together on the same side of an issue."

State groups have also worked on projects to aid undocumented aliens, the resettlement of refugees, and Indian ministries. There seem to be some critical issues that can best be addressed by a mission-centered ecumenical body that covers an entire state. Whether state conferences and councils of churches are alive and well or not, there is a perceived need for the ministry they can accomplish.

Campus Ministries

Another dimension of ecumenical cooperation has been in campus ministries, but the degree of commitment varies from state to state. In some places United Methodism has preferred to maintain a denominational identity. Elsewhere it has been felt that resources could be used more wisely by sponsoring ministries jointly with other denominations through United Ministries in Higher Education (UMHE).

Campus ministers who work ecumenically testify to the value of the latter arrangements. Says one, "Working in the higher education scene is perhaps much like working in the Third-World missionary environment: Denominational distinctions mean very little to many of the students, faculty, and staff. In addition to our five sponsoring bodies—United Methodist, United Presbyterian, United Church of Christ, American Baptist, and Disciples of Christ—I also try to work in coalition with Roman Catholics and Lutherans."

Working on state college campuses means coming up against church/state conflicts. "It's easier for the university administration to deal with us as an ecumenical ministry; they feel less pressured than if it's a single denomination, because they can say they're giving all of us equal opportunity."

There can be complications in working ecumenically: "The farther away one gets in the chain of accountability from sources of money, the less commitment and personal involvement there is from those sources. I am subject to a local board which is accountable to the state UMHE commission. It is accountable to a series of denominational boards, and those boards are accountable to their denominations. That's quite a chain. There's a certain credibility gap between those involved day to day and those removed. It's quite a removal by the time you get back to the denomination."

A district superintendent senses "more and more questions being raised about ecumenical campus ministry involvements. Some people have a concern that there needs to be a local-church-based ministry. Part of the concern is the money crunch: We're giving the most support financially, and there's the feeling that we're doing more than our share."

No clear consensus exists in the denomination in favor of either a United Methodist or an ecumenical campus ministry. It is probable that both kinds of ministries will continue to coexist, with ecumenical efforts being more common on campuses where United Methodists cannot afford to fund a ministry by themselves, or where a genuine commitment exists. Ministry with a United Methodist sponsorship will be maintained when it is felt to be the most effective means of reaching United Methodist students.

The whole debate about ecumenical campus ministry takes place in the context of shifting styles in campus ministry. There is a growing recognition that maintaining such a presence at only large four-year universities may be an elitist use of resources. Increased attention is now being given to providing such a ministry to junior colleges, community colleges, and to vocational and technical schools. The great increase of middle-aged students makes different demands upon campus ministries than did the traditional emphasis on students just out of high school. In coming decades, the decline in the number of students reaching "college age" will call for further reevaluation of the involvements of churches in campus work.

Seminaries

Since theological education is a significant factor in determining clergy attitudes toward ecumenism, it is important to ask, How ecumenically committed are United Methodist seminaries? Faculty and staff generally will assert that their schools are very ecumenical, as shown by the interdenominational makeup of faculties and student bodies, their reciprocal arrangements for cross-registration and library sharing with other nearby seminaries, their curriculum, and the minimizing of denominational membership requirements for trustee boards.

Still, many United Methodists *perceive* that seminaries and seminary faculty are less interested in ecumenical studies now than they were a few years ago. The influence of teachers of ecumenics can be significant. Many seminary graduates credit a particular professor with having generated an excitement about ecumenism: "The dean of our school was fully a participant in the ecumenical movement. He saw to it that ecumenical leadership from all places in the world came through our campus and talked with us. My fascination with ecumenism came through the lives of those persons whom I saw as fully able to bridge all kinds of barriers."

Some persons feel they must go to an ecumenical seminary to have such experiences. A woman graduate says, "The nondenominational seminary I went to had a faculty and student body representing all kinds of denominations. The worship service, theology—all of it was very ecumenical. It was very much an experience of learning about other traditions."

Even those United Methodist seminaries thought by some to be not very ecumenical are accused by others of hiring too many non-Methodist faculty members, trying too hard to attract big-name Roman Catholic scholars, and putting insufficient emphasis on the business of training United Methodists to serve United Methodism.

The two United Methodist seminaries most often mentioned as being especially ecumenical are Gammon Theological Seminary, because it is part of the Interdenominational Theological Center in Atlanta, and The School of Theology at Claremont (California), which has Episcopal and Disciples components and deliberately maintains a strongly ecumenical focus. But a school that seeks to be ecumenical is often criticized. Says one churchman about Claremont, "They overprioritized ecumenism. They made the school so ecumenical that it lost its United Methodist focus and United Methodist support dropped. It has affected fund raising. You've got to be visibly United Methodist to get United Methodist money."

In most or all of the United Methodist seminaries, one can find individual faculty members, both United Methodist and non-United Methodist, who are deeply committed to ecumenism and who work at transmitting an ecumenical consciousness to their students. By no means are these persons to be found teaching only ecumenics. They may be specialists in worship, church history, missions, social ethics, Old Testament, or some other discipline. But in addition to the inspiration of individual ecumenically minded professors, what is needed, say many ecumenists, is the commitment of a seminary as a whole to the ecumenical enterprise.

General Agencies

The extent to which the denomination's general agencies work ecumenically varies enormously, depending partly on the nature of their work.

The agency with the most extensive functions in this regard is, of course, the General Commission on Christian Unity and Interreligious Concerns. When the 1980 General Conference removed this division from the General Board of Global Ministries and transformed it into a freestanding commission, the action was widely viewed as a boon to ecumenism. It gave the agency, its personnel, and the whole ecumenical endeavor more visibility churchwide. It did the same at the annual conference level for the related commissions, which now have representation on conference councils on ministry. As a separate agency, the general commission is perceived as having more power, influence, and importance.

The Book of Discipline of The United Methodist Church assigns specific ecumenical functions to some general agencies; *The Discipline* is silent on this point in the case of other agencies. For example, the Board of Higher Education and Ministry, according to *The Discipline,* is responsible for developing and maintaining "cooperative relationships with ecumenical agencies and other denominations for the full discharge of the objectives of the Board." The Board of Discipleship is given authority "to provide representation in ecumenical and interdenominational agencies as they relate to the work of the board."

An agency such as the General Council on Ministries, which has coordinating, oversight, and accountability functions in relation to other United Methodist agencies, would have few cooperative responsibilities dealing specifically with other denominations. On the other hand, the Board of Church and Society, in providing "forthright witness and action" on social issues, often has occasion to enter into networks and coalitions with other church bodies.

Some of the work of general agencies is accomplished by going through the cognate units of the National Council of Churches. For example, the United Methodist Committee on Relief (a division of the Board of Global Ministries) works closely with the NCC's relief arm, Church World Service. Some ecumenical involvements take the form of ad hoc interdenominational coalitions. For example, the Board of Higher Education and Ministry cooperated with twenty-two denominations in a Congress on Church-Related Colleges and Universities, to develop common strategies for survival.

Church agencies that hold stock in corporations often form interreligious coalitions, together with Catholic religious orders, to bring pressure on companies in regard to unethical or inhumane corporate policies or practices by presenting resolutions at annual shareholder meetings. For example, such pressure has been brought on firms that do business in South Africa.

The communications agencies of some of the churches in COCU, primarily the United Methodist and the Disciples, have experimented with sharing their staff people for news coverage of denominational meetings. Disciples staff worked in the United Methodist newsroom at General Conference, and a United Methodist staff member helped with coverage of the Disciples General Assembly.

General agency ecumenical involvements also include such things as:

• Sharing of information and resources across denominational lines.

• Joining in friend-of-the-court briefs on court cases involving church/state issues. Agencies of several denominations took such action recently in a case involving the Worldwide Church of God and state officials in California.

• Sponsoring joint consultations on issues of mutual interest, such as church/state issues.

• Issuing joint statements aimed at influencing public policy. It is felt such statements have greater impact because they represent several denominations.

• Organizing networks and coalitions to provide information, lobby in legislatures, influence public opinion, and build citizen support for a certain course of action.

These examples only scratch the surface. At present, there

are dozens of ways in which general agencies are working ecumenically. Undoubtedly many further opportunities for such collaboration have yet to be explored and developed. One can envision that instead of each denomination undertaking the expense of publishing its own hymnal, there could be a cooperatively published ecumenical hymnal. The Canadian churches have given us an example of such a venture with the 1971 hymnbook produced jointly by the Anglican Church of Canada and the United Church of Canada.

The current cooperation seen in *A.D.*, a general-interest church magazine published jointly by The United Presbyterian Church and the United Church of Christ, might also be a model for the future. One can imagine that United Methodists, who have had no official all-church magazine since the demise of *Together* and its successor *Today,* might consider entering into such a cooperative enterprise with other denominations.

Despite the many examples of interdenominational information sharing, churches often seem to be reinventing the wheel when they undertake studies of critical issues. The question of homosexuality and ordination arose at about the same time in several Protestant denominations. Virtually every one of those churches launched its own extensive and expensive study process. For the sake of efficiency and economy, it would seem to make sense for cooperative studies to be undertaken interdenominationally, when several bodies are concerned with the same questions.

The really daring step in collaboration of agencies across denominatonal lines will come when those units begin to work so closely together that it is possible to merge structures, with a joint agency serving two or more denominations. This would not be merger for the sake of merger, but for the sake of mission.

Despite the disciplinary mandates directing one general agency or another to maintain cooperative ecumenical working relationships, no consensus is yet present in the church for establishing a denominational policy directing all agencies to examine all their responsibilities in the light of ecumenical principles, working ecumenically wherever it is practical and beneficial to do so. In the absence of pressure from the local churches for such General Conference action, it is not likely that many general agencies will establish this policy on their own. Indeed, countervailing forces encourage agencies to "think United Methodist," rather than "think ecumenical." And such local church pressure will not be forthcoming without widespread understanding of the practical benefits of such a policy. Many fruitful opportunities for ecumenical rapprochement at the agency level await discovery.

Summary

By now, it should be clear to the reader that ecumenism is not one thing, but many; not a narrow category, but a multifaceted array of relationships, having implications for practically everything United Methodists do. In ecumenical agencies at world, national, state, and metropolitan levels; in seminaries that shape the church's spiritual leaders; on college and university campuses; in theological conversations; and in the action-oriented collaboration of church agencies—at all levels of the church, United Methodists are finding ecumenism to be not only possible, but necessary.

Lack of awareness, on the part of members and pastors, of the variety of ecumenical activities beyond the local church suggests a vital task for the denomination's present and future. Despite United Methodism's connectional linkages, the lines of communication are not as effective as they need to be. Local church people must be informed of the magnitude of the ecumenical enterprise and the way it is serving the interests of the local church. Finding ways to ensure that the story is heard should be a priority assignment for ecumenically committed leaders of the church.

CHAPTER 8

Key Influences:
Boosts and Barriers

Earlier chapters have examined motives for ecumenical involvement. But whatever United Methodists' motives and intentions, certain factors will affect the ecumenical atmosphere for good or for ill. This chapter will discuss several factors that will either enhance or discourage the possibilities for ecumenical activity.

• *The Role of the Pastor.* Both clergy and laity speak of the local church pastor as being the single most important influence for ecumenical activity. The pastor is seen as a gatekeeper who decides what information gets through from other levels to local church members. "The local pastor is the communicator," says one minister. "I do not see any way around that. He or she is the key to communications, and to a very great extent, to the attitudes and direction in which the congregation goes." A lay church worker observes: "In most of the churches I've worked in, the pastor can make or break any program. He can educate his people, and the majority will go along with him, because he's their leader and they respect that."

What are the implications for ecumenism in the pastor's leading role? First, in many cases, ecumenical bodies and denominational agencies, practically speaking, have no access to the laity without the pastor. If many lay people say, for example, that they have never heard of COCU, one reason may be that their pastors have not talked about it. If the pastor is a block to the transmission of positive images of ecumenism, few alternate routes are available for reaching those in the pews.

Second, if one wanted to circumvent the pastor, it could be more easily done if there were a denominational publication that would reach most families. At present, even the widely circulated but independent *United Methodist Reporter,* which has become the de facto news organ of the church, does not come close to reaching every home. Moreover, as an unofficial publication, the *Reporter* has no obligation to advocate any particular approach to ecumenism or any official stance of the denomination.

• *Frequency of Pastoral Moves.* Because of United Methodism's itineracy system, its clergy probably move from one pastorate to the next more frequently than do ministers of other denominations. Some ecumenists view this mobility as a liability in building strong ecumenical relationships. "How can you really be part of a community if you have to move every four or five years?" asks one leader.

One laywoman observes that grass-roots coalitions often arise as a result of trust and friendship among clergy in neighborhood churches. When there is a change of pastors, the trust must be rebuilt, the informal covenant renegotiated. A pastor who was involved in one of COCU's local Interim Eucharistic Fellowships testifies that the experiment "fizzled out because it was too dependent on clerical leadership. Within a twenty-month period, five of the seven pastors who originally had participated moved or were transferred. The incoming pastors did not have that much interest." Such statements may suggest the crucial need for continuous, strong, self-starting lay leadership in a system where frequent changes of clergy leadership occur.

• *Personal Friendships.* As suggested above, many ecumenical involvements are initiated as a result of friendships between persons in the participating denominations. Many pastors seem to have cultivated friendships with colleagues in other communions out of personal need for emotional support or because of mutual interests and compatibility, and they have built on these friendships to bring their congregations into a state of ecclesiastical friendship. That in turn has led to the budding of personal friendships between members of the churches. "It starts one to one," says a Western Jurisdiction pastor. "One pastor of one church becomes a friend and caring partner with another minister in another church, and that carries on to others in the church."

• *Visionary Leadership.* While ecumenism-as-cooperation has considerable support among the denomination's pragmatists, the pursuit of Christian unity in the form of organic church union continues only because of the presence of a small but determined band committed to a vision that most others do not see. The ecumenical true believers are a small minority, and many of them are in the over-fifty generations. If the concerns they represent are to continue to be voiced, it is important that they transmit their vision to younger people—a task that has implications for seminary curriculum, campus ministries, youth programs, church school literature, and confirmation materials, among other things.

• *The Information Overload.* Church folk are inundated with so much reading material from so many sources that much of it is never digested. Pastors and active lay members lead busy lives. There is a continuous stream of new books from both religious and secular presses that one could read for spiritual or theological growth. There is also the need to keep up with magazines and newspapers, not to mention informational material from church agencies. In pastors' studies all over the country, one can see desks stacked with unread annual conference and general church mailing pieces, awaiting the pastor's catch-up reading time.

If information from ecumenical agencies is to get through, it will need to be presented in a fashion that competes with the wealth of other printed material vying for attention. A pastor says, "My gut-level response when I received this booklet from COCU was, 'Well, that's kind of a nice thing, but I've got so many other things I need to deal with.' "

A district superintendent says, "This COCU document is not written in lay language."

One district superintendent suggests that one way to bypass the information overload is to provide "warm bodies to talk about church union. There's no way to catch the vision of the enthusiasm and the importance when you read a piece of paper. The people who are involved need to be talking about it at the local level."

• *Press Distortions.* Fairly or unfairly, many ecumenists blame the press (both religious and secular) and broadcast media for misinterpreting ecumenical actions. Ecumenical effectiveness is seen as being damaged by careless or sensational reporting. At one time, "it was almost a conspiracy of the religious press," charges an ecumenical leader, "to advance the slogan 'COCU Is Dead.' Statements like that have a devastating effect."

More recently, secular press reports about a "nonsexist Bible" brought a torrent of angry letters to the National Council of Churches officials, who were then faced with the task of sending out accurate information to church people, explaining what sort of task its committee of Bible scholar-translators actually was engaged in.

Does the press "get it wrong"? Or is it a case of overreaction by the denominations? Is there a consistent pattern of distortion by the press? These issues have yet to be adequately explored. Closer communication between church leaders and media people might be beneficial and yield some remedies.

• *Issues That Fracture the Fellowship.* Ecumenical relationships have been broken by controversy in many communities where previously there was harmonious cooperation on a wide variety of issues. Currently, the issue that most often causes fracture is abortion. A United Methodist pastor says, "When our bishop came out for prochoice, the Catholics pulled all support out of a joint project. This one issue was so divisive that the Roman Catholics said, 'We will not cooperate on anything.'" To a lesser extent, differing views on aid to nonpublic schools, or state gambling laws that permit church bingo games can erode amicable relationships between Catholics and Protestants. Strong opposing opinions on the Israeli-Palestinian conflict and affirmative action programs have created hard feelings between Jews and black Christians who previously had cooperated on common concerns.

• *The Press of Priorities.* Time and finances for programs and activities of local churches, annual conferences, and the general church take priority over ecumenical endeavors. A laywoman expresses it this way: "Most clergy are having to struggle with their own situation, and practically, they don't have the energy for things beyond the local church. They are trying to hold the local church together, keep it in operation." It is widely felt that every year, more and more demands are made upon the time and energy of the pastor and the active lay leadership of congregations.

The implication of this situation is that unless ecumenical cooperation somehow means sharing the total burden, rather than adding an extra task, the practical commitment to working ecumenically will not increase.

• *A Sense of Connectionalism.* Despite the fact that theirs is a connectional church, many United Methodists tend to think congregationally rather than conectionally. In most congregations, only a few persons become sufficiently involved in structures beyond the local level to urge upon others a consciousness of the larger dimensions of their church.

But thinking connectionally does seem to be an intermediate step toward thinking ecumenically. The local church that forms no cooperative linkages with other United Methodist congregations is not likely to form such linkages with non-United Methodist churches. Many speak interchangeably of relating to other United Methodist congregations and of relating to non-United Methodist groups, as though these were basically the same kind of relationship. In some instances, unfortunately, congregations seem to use connectionalism as a substitute for ecumenism, or as an excuse for not being ecumenical.

• *Bishops Are Basic.* Just as the pastor is the key figure at the local level, bishops individually are seen as the key influences in the annual conferences, and bishops collectively play that role at the general church level. Opinions differ as to how genuinely committed the Council of Bishops as a whole has been to Christian unity, although a recent upsurge in interest has been noted in the strengthening of relationships with their counterparts in the three black Methodist denominations. A bishop can play a significant role in motivating local church pastors through his or her own active involvement in ecumenical activities.

• *Size As a Factor.* It's easier to be pragmatically ecumenical when you are small. Small-membership churches are more likely to realize that "we need each other." Large churches with the resources to "do it ourselves" are less likely to realize their need for others. This observation applies to individual congregations, to the totality of United Methodism in one location—as in a town, a metropolitan area, or a state—and to the denomination. Perhaps the message here for prosperous large churches, for powerful annual conferences, for United Methodists in areas where they are one of the dominant churches, and for the total denomination, is that pragmatism has its limits; that smaller, less affluent denominations need the participation of United Methodists in ecumenical endeavors; that a church is not truly "being ecumenical" when it always asks, What's in it for us?

• *A Bridging Role.* United Methodists, in the midst of mainline Protestantism, may be uniquely equipped to play an ecumenical role as a bridge denomination between evangelical bodies and liturgical bodies such as Lutheran, Episcopal, and Catholic. United Methodism has been characterized as being bland but grand, lacking a clear public identity despite being one of the country's largest churches. But perhaps it is this seeming blandness that allows a riotous profusion of races, cultures, ideologies, theologies, and life-styles to coexist in more or less peaceful pluralism. Indeed, so theologically pluralistic are United Methodists that they may be said already to embody an ecumenism within their own denomination. We know United Methodism is often the compromise denomination for married couples, when one is a Baptist and the other an Episcopalian or Catholic. When such couples who demonstrate an ecumenism within their own marriages and family life are added to the fellowship, they not only provide models for compromise and acceptance of differences, but also add to the richness and diversity of United Methodism. United Methodists, because of their "middleness" and their internal diversities, are strategically placed for looking to both right and left in their ecumenical outreach. This moderation and adaptability may be significant in enabling the denomination's readiness for ecumenical rapprochement.

• *Mobility of Population.* Denominational labels are becoming less important for many laity, partly because of the highly mobile nature of our population. Many people who move to a new community join a church not because it is "their" denomination, but because a friend, relative, or neighbor invited them to come; because they like its church school, its music, its youth program, its pastor; because it is in their neighborhood.

Laity are more likely than clergy to view denominational differences as relatively unimportant. Says a Texas pastor, "The laity today aren't hung up on denominations, but on finding a church where they feel loved. They don't come here because we're United Methodists. They come because we love 'em. They come because they have a basic need to be affirmed."

A pastor in the Southeastern Jurisdiction says, "I don't hear people saying, 'We've always been Methodists.' They're saying, 'Well, we were Baptists in Charlotte, Presbyterians in Greensboro, and we might as well be Methodists here, if the church is friendly.' It's an odd sort of ecumenism by default. We take in as many non-Methodists as Methodists. People are being sort of consumers about this thing."

It would be fair to surmise that perhaps as many of these

consumers find happiness among the Presbyterians or Baptists as with United Methodists. As far as church growth is concerned, United Methodism can either gain or lose from the tendency to blur denominational identity, depending on the kind of nourishment it offers the hungering churchgoer. But from an ecumenical perspective, it may be a healthy tendency. There is perhaps no way to measure it scientifically, but many people have a hunch that the ex-Lutherans, ex-Baptists, ex-Catholics, and ex-Presbyterians in their midst are one factor in the laity's openness to Christian unity. These nomadic Christians who migrate from one denomination to another are acting out in their own lives the belief that the Church is one, though more cynical observers may suggest that it is only the not-so-committed who do not care about denominational differences.

• *The New Religious Right and the Electronic Church.* Two major, and to some extent related, phenomena recently have had an impact on mainline ecumenism. The Moral Majority and similar religiopolitical organizations of the New Religious Right represent a kind of right-wing ecumenism. They are a linkage of religious people of various denominations. However, this linkage is seen by many mainline religionists as demonic in the way it seeks to define the public good and to impose its own moral definitions on the society.

The electronic church, though its various evangelists claim to be nondenominational, turns out to be not ecumenical, but paradenominational—that is, having some of the characteristics of a denomination. But the electronic church is not a community of faith. Its viewers do not interact in community with one another. The only "community" they share is that of being on the same mailing list in some television evangelist's computer bank.

Some observers say the success of electronic religion and Religious Right politics is causing mainline Protestants to realize that they need one another—that they must get together in new ecumenical coalitions to work for common interests and to fight dangerous tendencies in public life and church/state relations. Moderates in evangelical denominations such as the Southern Baptist Convention, eager to put some distance between themselves and their fundamentalist brothers and sisters, may be in need of allies and may develop a new openness to cooperation with mainline religionists.

A Washington, D.C., minister sees the New Religious Right giving mainline Protestants a new appreciation of denominationalism. "Jerry Falwell would say he is accountable to the gospel. But I see him being accountable to a computer in Falls Church, Virginia, and to his Nielsen and Arbitron ratings. That is different from being accountable to a synod, a diocese, an annual conference, a presbytery. All of a sudden, I have seen the importance of a line of accountability to a judicatory with democratically observed procedures."

United Methodists will differ as to whether the electronic church and the New Religious Right are a threat to mainline interests and the ecumenical enterprise. Perhaps it can be agreed, however, that the rise of right-wing religiopolitics offers a challenge and makes clear the need for United Methodism and its colleague churches to define more clearly the appropriate relationship between their common witness and the political order. And the electronic religionists make clear to ecumenical-minded churches the untapped possibilities for witness to secular society through the medium of television.

• *Divergent Definitions.* A difference within United Methodism in defining ecumenism may be symptomatic of a deep division in ecumenical strategy. A laywoman complains, "The laity *want* to be ecumenical. But our pastor insists that everything has to have a United Methodist label on it—every outside speaker, every mission project, every piece of Sunday school literature. Anything else is regarded as off-brand." A spokesman from United Methodism's evangelical wing, writing in *Good News,* argues that the denomination's support of ecumenical groups "provides strong precedent for evangelicals to support missionaries who are not exclusively United Methodist. We are glad that real United Methodists do not regard the Kingdom's limits as our own denominational borders."

What about the church school teachers who want to use David C. Cook literature, instead of Nashville's; the local church laity who want to give mission funds to World Gospel Mission or to Wycliffe Bible Translators, rather than channeling money through the Board of Global Ministries? Is there something to be said for this free-lance approach to ecumenism?

Some denominational leaders may respond, "But that's not being ecumenical. That's just being antidenominational and seeking to undermine United Methodist programs of mission and Christian education. That's being anticonnectional." They may also remind the questioner that the proceeds from the sale of United Methodist church school literature helps pay ministerial pensions. Is one being ecumenical if one's actions have the effect of being antidenominational?

Is there a good ecumenism and a bad ecumenism? Shall we seek to contain the ecumenical spirit solely in official structures and channels? This is an era of burgeoning "parachurch" groups (*para:* "closely resembling the true form") in the areas of missions, Bible translation, campus ministry, publishing. What are the implications of the fact that United Methodists have no guidelines for relating ecumenically to a not-quite-a-church? Are such organizations a part of Christendom? United Methodists have scarcely begun to wrestle with the way such questions may affect their ecumenical future.

Summary

Leadership, communications, mobility, identity, competition—these are among the factors that may either inspire or discourage the pursuit of Christian unity. The findings described in this chapter suggest that The United Methodist

Church may need to: (a) give more attention to the education of pastors in the ecumenical mandates of the gospel; (b) fix longer tenures for pastoral appointments; (c) establish concerted communications programs in regard to ecumenical commitments; (d) consult with Roman Catholics and others to bring about reconciliation in the face of fellowship-fracturing issues; (e) give greater attention to lay leadership development and training; (f) encourage more dialogue between liberal/ecumenical and conservative/evangelical elements within the denomination in regard to perceptions of the church's ecumenical mandate.

This is an important, though only a partial, list. There is no shortage of items for the ecumenical agenda.

CHAPTER 9

Economics and the 1980s

What will be the impact of the 1980s on ecumenical involvement? United Methodists generally agree that the United States is in an era of inflation, shrinking resources, and rising energy costs and that these trends may continue. It will cost more to build new church buildings; heating and cooling will be more expensive. The remainder of the century is likely to be an era of trying to do more with less. What effect this will have on ecumenical endeavors is not yet clear. Most observers believe that the church has not reached the crunch point of economic hardship and that most church people are not ready to acknowledge that dramatic changes may be in the offing.

Our interviewees saw three possible scenarios.

1. Ecumenical cooperation will continue at essentially the present level. Even with fuel shortages and inflation, local churches will not become more open to sharing facilities but will continue to prefer to do their own thing, maintain their own turf. United Methodists will continue to pay their share of ecumenical budgets and will express the same reasons for doing so that they always have.

2. Because of economic pressures, churches will pull back from any ecumenical cooperation that involves a financial commitment. When budget cuts become necessary, ecumenical activities will be among the first things regarded as dispensable. As a consequence, denominational programs and local church budgets will reflect a retreat to self-interest and survival.

3. Because of rising costs, local churches will be more open

to sharing of resources and facilities. More local congregations of differing denominations will build joint facilities and share existing space, staff, equipment, and other resources. Denominational judicatories and agencies will work more cooperatively than ever before to avoid duplication of effort in missions, publishing, and curriculum design.

Evidence for the first scenario is found especially in the South, Southwest, and West, where people are inclined to say, "Things will have to get pretty bad before there would be much difference in the way we operate." One pastor says that "it's got to be a very serious energy crisis to overcome the local church's sense of turf. Maybe here's where some of the gap is—between the theologians who dream the dream of unity and the local churchgoers who love their church. I don't know if the theologians have a real sense of what kind of emotional investment laity have in their church building. It's their holy place." A Nevadan adds, "There always seems to be another nickel to keep a United Methodist church open. Sharing facilities sounds good in theory, but there's not much interest in actually doing it."

Energy-saving ideas are talked about, and there are a few energy task forces around, but not much is being accomplished. The things that *are* being done focus on the local church—insulating, and using its heating plant more efficiently. "Churches needing to save on heating bills will generally prefer to meet in the basement for winter, rather than heat up a high-ceilinged sanctuary. They will do this rather than share a building."

There is also evidence for the second scenario, the pullback from ecumenical commitment. Annual conference officials in several areas say that councils of churches and cooperative agencies at the middle judicatory level are already hurting for funds because the United Methodist annual conferences and analogous decision-making bodies in other denominations have reduced funding. Says one official, "When any economic threat arises, we'll pull back support from an ecumenical service project to maintain a denominational project." Another observer: "When the crunch comes, ecumenism is one of the first things to go." A conference staff director puts it bluntly: "Ecumenism is a luxury. It's peripheral. It's nice if we can do it, but increasingly, we don't have the staff time or the dollars, so that's what gets cut."

A South Carolinian observes, "There's a survival mentality. It's getting tight all over. We're trimming budgets. I'm afraid the ecumenical business seems like a luxury. We're no longer negotiating from a position of strength. Anything we do feels like a declining denomination grasping for something. That's just not a happy climate for ecumenism."

As for the third scenario, there may be some hopeful signs in new church development, though some flickers of interest have failed to ignite. In South Carolina, a Presbyterian and a United Methodist church considered building a multipurpose unit together. However, "the idea has not come to realization." In Wisconsin, a thirty-member United Methodist church talked with a Baptist congregation about sharing facilities during the winter months. An observer of that situation says, "They may need to merge for their life and health and witness in that community." Again, the idea was considered and, while it also has not come to be, at least some folks are thinking "ecumenism."

In many parts of the country, yoked parishes are a fact of life for survival. An ecumenist explains: "We cannot afford to pay salaries and pensions for pastors of churches of 50 to 100 members. How can we justify half-filled churches competing across the street from each other?"

There are a few examples of churches that have successfully shared facilities. In Wisconsin, an Episcopalian and a United Methodist congregation each needed a building at the same time. They built together, not because it was an economic necessity, but because it was a way for both to save money and to act ecumenically. Many observers note that the biggest changes in willingness to share space, resources, and staff arise from an economic concern, not from a sense of stewardship or an idealistic desire to consume less of the world's resources. As one ecumenist observes, "God uses secondary motivation rather frequently."

A campus minister stresses that "even when ecumenism is pragmatic, we still have a Christian witness to bear. Even if the sharing of buildings to reduce energy costs is begun because a congregation could not afford its energy bills, it is also a witness to the rest of the world, which is also suffering from the energy crisis."

Can the church's response to the energy crisis and inflation be a model for the future? One minister declares, "I don't think there's any other institution in our society that's going to be able to deal with this era of scarcity in a humane way, educating people in terms of values other than materialism and consumption. The church must be a model."

The right questions about stewardship and practical economics are being raised, though sometimes timidly. The impact of economic factors on ecumenical commitments is not yet known. Economics and ecumenics in the 1980s may well be on a converging course, and United Methodists may discover that theology and pragmatism are pointing in the same direction.

CHAPTER 10

The Making of an Ecumenist

The United Methodist Church enters American Methodism's third century at a time of change and anxiety both for society and for religious institutions. Inflationary pressures and economic uncertainty threaten to impose drastic changes in ecclesiastical standards of living, while a few prophetic voices are calling for voluntary changes in church patterns of consumption.

For several years membership figures for The United Methodist Church have been declining. With fewer young people joining mainline Protestant churches, United Methodism may be becoming a church for the middle-aged. Clergy morale is sagging. With secularism growing on one side and conservative religion on the other, some observers see a collapse of the "middle" and a loss of vitality in the major denominations.

A common observation is that "the ecumenical *spirit* is flourishing; but the ecumenical *movement* is in disarray." That situation is not unconnected to economics. In the postwar years of the 1950s, both the churches and the economy were booming. The mood was expansive and generous—and the ecumenical movement blossomed as never before. As the economy has worsened and the national mood has turned wary and ungenerous, ecumenical institutions have come under attack and suffered from loss of momentum and enthusiasm. Is there a connection between a sense of prosperity and well being and the ability to reach out beyond one's religious "tribe" to embrace a large community? Is there a correlation between an income diminished by inflation and an ecumenicism diminished by inwardness and parochialism?

One can predict that the churches' response to whatever economic crises may come will be pragmatic and survival-oriented, as well as activist and mission-minded. But one cannot predict whether that response will be to conserve economic resources by spending less on ecumenical involvements, or whether the churches will be imaginative enough to see collaboration in common programming with colleague churches as a way of doing more with less. At present, working closely together is often hindered by the various brands of bureaucratic red tape that must be reckoned with. The churches will need to be committed to making cooperation easier by enabling church legislation and by developing a spirit of flexibility and an understanding of one another's structure and polity.

Denominations are not likely to "major" in innovative ecumenical practices in a time of retrenchment and austerity, unless three necessary components are present: (a) committed passionate leadership, with a vision of the wholeness of the Body of Christ; (b) effective communication strategies within and among denominations; and (c) denominational consensus of "left" and "right" on the meaning of Christian unity and the priority of its pursuit in the scheme of things.

A New Generation of Leadership

Sometimes what people do not say is as significant as what they do say. After transcribing hours of taped conversations with clergy and laity, this author was struck by the realization that virtually nothing had been said to indicate that children and youth in local churches are being deliberately exposed to ecumenical experiences and an ecumenical view of the church. One small-town pastor did speak of a cooperative vacation Bible school that gathers up all the kids in town—Methodist, Baptist, Presbyterian, and all. But by and large, the formative experiences that United Methodist children are receiving seem not to include a strong ecumenical component in church schools, vacation church schools, confirmation classes, or youth groups.

Interestingly, however, the more enthusiastic ecumenists, most of whom are middle-aged or older, typically said that their commitment to Christian unity grew out of a particular ecumenical experience. They often mentioned their experiences with some ecumenical youth or student group, often an international one. The large gatherings sponsored by such groups made a memorable impression on the then young people who participated.

The great ecumenical youth conferences seem to have withered away. One hears periodically that ecumenical student movements are about to be revived, but for the time being, that activity seems to have been ceded to the conservative, evangelical parachurch groups such as InterVarsity. The current generation of United Methodist youth and young adults is not experiencing the invigorating and eye-opening ecumenical opportunities their elders had.

If commitment to Christian unity grows out of exposure and experience, then can a new generation of leadership be produced without such encounters? Will the next generation of clergy be as ecumenically inclined as the pastors who talk today about the seminary professors who aroused their enthusiasm? Theological schools will need to be mindful of their responsibility for the formation of ecumenical-minded leaders for the church. The ecumenical spirit may flower naturally without cultivation in the laity, but at some point, that diffuse and abstract spirit must find concrete embodiment in institutions, if it is to bear fruit. If The United Methodist Church is to continue to live out its articulated commitment to openness, it must give more attention to the nurture of ecumenism in its members and leaders—through the church school, confirmation classes, youth groups, seminaries, lay speakers' training, adult Christian education, and the education that takes place during worship. Unless the making of ecumenists is a task seriously undertaken, there will be no one in the coming generation to take up the cause as the present generation of leaders passes from the scene.

Communications

To be equipped to assume ecumenical leadership, church members must be supplied with the information they need. In a speech to a division of the National Council of Churches, Arie Brouwer of the Reformed Church in America said, "I'm convinced that today, more than ever, the quality of our community life is dependent on the quality of our communication." He went on to say that the involvement of church journalists and communicators must begin at the point where policies are conceived—not after the fact.

All this assumes that communicators speak in the language of the laity and are in touch with the constituency. If one examines the failure of ecumenical institutions to win support at the grass roots, these failures are, to a great extent, ones of communication. Either the word is not reaching the people at all, or it is reaching them without adequate interpretation. Through reporting news, providing interpretation and analyses, offering criticism or a word of advocacy, church communicators have a vital role in the ecumenical enterprise. But their ability to play that role depends upon church strategies, policies, and funding levels which acknowledge the crucial necessity of communications.

Left and Right

In listening to the people of the denomination, one hears a disturbing assumption in language that uses *evangelical* as a synonym for *conservative,* and *ecumenical* as a synonym for *liberal.* No wonder the denomination's evangelistic outreach is in trouble, if evangelism is considered the private province of one portion of the church! No wonder our ecumenism is irrelevant, if it ignores everyone who is to the right of center. What is needed is a theology and practice that bind together evangelical and ecumenical. How about an *ecumenical evangelism?* Or an *evangelical ecumenism?*

In *The Public Church,* Martin Marty defines *public church* as a "communion of communions, each of which lives its life partly in response to its separate tradition and partly to the calls for a common Christian vocation." The phrase *communion of communions* has come to suggest an emerging but not yet defined vision of a pattern, or form, to embody both the unity and the diversity of the church. Bringing that blurred vision into sharp focus will be the task of coming decades.

Our era is one in which localism and grass-roots power are cherished; bigness and bureaucracy and centralized power are distrusted. Church union efforts will fail if the uneasiness about centralization is not addressed, whatever proposed structural arrangement emerges.

Much dialogue will be needed within The United Methodist Church, and within the whole Christian community, on the meaning of church unity. United Methodism's own internal divisions and differences between left and right may in fact be a more serious "scandal of disunity." The first ecumenical task is to build a sense of unity and a consensus of direction within the denomination. As long as the quest for Christian unity is seen as being for liberals only, the movement will not proceed closer to its goal. Church people who disagree on capitalism, socialism, abortion, the role of women, affirmative action strategies, gay rights, liberation theology, and biblical authority must acknowledge that they are one in Christ.

Ways must be devised for living together as members of that group called United Methodists, and then for moving beyond denominationalism to manifest the oneness to which they are called. A time of talking and listening and of imaging the future is needed now. If such a process were made a quadrennial emphasis or an all-church priority, we might then see a quadrennium of conversation, a four-year-long dialogue aimed at bringing some clarity to the church's ecumenical intentions for its third century.

It may be necessary for both liberals and conservatives to give up some of their most cherished presuppositions about the ecumenical future. Left and right and middle, bishops and bureaucrats, pastors and pew-sitters, grass-roots Christians and power people—all must be involved in determining United Methodism's ecumenical future. All must be helped to glimpse those faint signs of the health and wholeness that are God's gift to a broken Church. And all the gifts of every one of God's pragmatic people called United Methodists must be used in the task of devising practical strategies for living out the implication of Christ's prayer "that they may all be one."

CPSIA information can be obtained at www.ICGtesting.com
Printed in the USA
LVOW101146080412

276640LV00001B/5/A